PUBLIC SCHOOLS

PUBLIC SCHOOLS

Issues in Budgeting and Financial Management

Edited by

John Augenblick

**The John D. and Catherine T. MacArthur
Foundation Symposium**

Transaction Books
New Brunswick (U.S.A.) and Oxford (U.K.)

Published by Transaction, Inc., 1985.
Copyright © 1985 by Public Financial Publications, Inc.

Library of Congress Catalog Number: 85-16364
ISBN: 0-88738-626-1 (paper)
Printed in the United States of America

Library of Congress Cataloging-in-Publication Data
Main entry under title:

Public schools.

    1. Education—United States—Finance—Addresses, essays, lectures. 2. Public schools—United States—Business management—Addresses, essays, lectures.
I. Augenblick, John.
LB2825.P84   1985   379.1'12'0973   85-16364
ISBN 0-88738-626-1 (pbk.) ⁄

This volume is sponsored by Public Financial Publications, Inc., the board of directors for *Public Budgeting & Finance*. Public Financial Publications is a nonprofit organization with financial support from the Section on Budgeting and Financial Management, American Society for Public Administration, and the American Association for Budget and Program Analysis.

The articles in this volume first appeared in the Winter 1984 and Spring 1985 issues of *Public Budgeting & Finance* as Parts I and II of a symposium sponsored by the John D. and Catherine T. MacArthur Foundation.

The John D. and Catherine T. MacArthur Foundation provided financial support to this volume.

Contents

Introduction: Elementary and Secondary Education—
Issues in Budgeting and Financial Management
    John Augenblick vii

The New Agenda for Education:
A Perspective for Policymakers
    Michael W. Kirst 1

State Government Contributions to the
Public Schools
    Charles S. Benson 11

State Aid for Local Schools:
Trends and Prospects
    Steven D. Gold 24

Providing Adequate Resources for Public
Elementary and Secondary Schools
    Richard H. Goodman 35

The Impact of Collective Bargaining on School
Management and Governance
    Michael J. Murphy 47

Emerging Roles of School District Administrators:
Implications for Planning, Budgeting, and
Management
    Guilbert C. Hentschke 59

Costs and Cost-Effectiveness of Computer-Assisted Instruction
    Henry M. Levin 71

Public School Closures and Policy Issues:
Financial and Social Implications
    Richard R. Valencia 87

JOHN AUGENBLICK

Introduction
Elementary and Secondary Education: Issues in Budgeting and Financial Management

For many people, even those involved in the education enterprise, school finance is a topic surrounded by some mystery. Citizens typically have no idea about the role of the state in funding local schools. Most legislators realize that education is the primary consumer of state general funds, but they are unfamiliar with the distribution mechanism. Many school administrators have so little knowledge about state finance systems that they are unable to predict how much they will receive. Not so long ago, the formulas used by states to allocate support to local school districts were the domain of only a few people, who understood both the mathematics and the politics involved. That situation changed somewhat in the last 15 years, in large part as a result of the effort to make school finance systems more equitable. Broad coalitions of legislators, educators, special interest groups, and citizens were formed; members of such coalitions learned about school finance and, aided by computers that could simulate the impacts of alternative systems, convinced legislatures to increase the sensitivity of aid distribution mechanisms to both the needs and fiscal capacities of school districts.

School finance systems have become more complex as they have become more precise about measuring pupil needs, determining the relative wealth of school districts, and assessing the costs of delivering education services. New approaches have been designed to provide more adequate funding, to distribute funds more equitably, and to promote local control over expenditure levels, tax rates, and how funds are spent. At the same time, states have taken a much larger role in funding schools. In most states, state aid is the largest single source of school revenue. Now, to a much greater extent than a decade ago, the future of the schools depends on the vitality of state revenue systems.

John Augenblick is a partner in Augenblick, Van de Water & Associates, a Denver-based consulting firm specializing in education finance, governance, and planning.

During the last few months, a new element has entered into discussions of school finance. A number of states have taken steps to improve the equality of their education systems. The cost of education is expected to increase as a result of changes such as raising teachers' salaries, creating career ladders or merit pay systems for teachers, lengthening the school day or the school year, modifying the curriculum, and testing both pupils and teachers. The first few states to implement some of these improvements last year also provided large sums of new money for education, usually by increasing taxes and earmarking part of the revenue for education.

It is questionable whether every state is capable of providing massive infusions of new funds or whether any state can continue to maintain such funding in the future. It is likely that states will move away from simply reimbursing districts for prior year expenditures, as is the case in many states now, and begin to provide explicit incentives to achieve various objectives, including school improvement and increased reliance on local property taxes. Policymakers generally recognize that all school finance systems provide incentives to school district administrators. In many cases, however, the incentives provided by state aid mechanisms were not consciously created; in some cases, the incentives that are provided run counter to certain educational objectives. The challenge for many states will be to design school finance systems that provide appropriate incentives for improvement while maintaining a high level of sensitivity to equity and local control.

Education is a labor-intensive industry. As such, the number of teachers employed and teacher salaries are important determinants of total cost. In a number of states, pupil-teacher ratios are important components of state aid formulas; however, most school finance systems are not driven by teacher salaries, although a number of states have statewide minimum salary schedules. During the past decade, teacher salaries and benefits have increased dramatically, in part due to the growth of local collective bargaining. States will need to be sensitive to these changes in order to assure that teachers are paid adequately and that salaries are equitable.

Another dimension of school improvement that has cost implications is the impact of technology on education. While personal computers are unlikely to replace teachers, they have proved useful in the classroom. Computer-assisted instruction, which has become a reality after two decades of expectation, has both benefits and costs. Also, it has become apparent that computers are not being distributed equitably across all school districts. The states will need to consider how they can use their school finance systems to assure that all pupils are exposed to and benefit from computers, computer-assisted instruction, expanding information bases, communications developments, and other products of technology.

One of the problems that has plagued school finance is the ability to assure that adequate resources are provided. No school finance system is an "entitlement" system that requires the state to allocate the amount specified by a statutory formula (although the state of Washington comes close). Most states use formulas to assure that available resources are distributed equitably. Despite the inability to demonstrate clear relationships between the availability of education resources and the production of achievement or any other education outcome, it is clear that districts that have more money do provide better services, in terms of teachers, materials, facilities, and other resources. A major concern of states is how to balance the need to control state expenditures against the desire to provide high quality education resources (and, hopefully, high quality education products). This tension will be resolved in school finance formulas.

The complexity of state aid systems and the rapidly changing education environment are likely to make the job of being a school administrator more difficult in the future. Education managers will face increasing pressure to demonstrate the effectiveness of the system. One of the most difficult tasks for school administrators is closing schools. Politically, it makes sense to retain the tradition of small local schools; however, for economic and educational reasons there is increasing pressure to eliminate small schools. Administrators will need to show that limited resources are being targeted to critical needs. Administrators will be required to deal with more parental involvement in the day-to-day operation of schools at the same time that a smaller proportion of the population has a direct interest in the schools. School administrators should become more knowledgeable about their school finance systems so that they can better project future funding, improve accountability, lobby for appropriate changes, and make their schools more effective.

MICHAEL W. KIRST

The New Agenda for Education:
A Perspective for Policymakers

There has been a virtual explosion of concern about the quality of American education in the last year. We may or may not have a rising tide of mediocrity, but there certainly is a rising tide of reports.[1] Indeed, this is a very brief period when education policy will be at center stage of national and state debates. The era 1983–85 will be for education somewhat similar to the era of the early 1970s for environmental issues. Recall the intense public interest after Earth Day about the environment. We will have perhaps three years of similar attention to education; our actions now will be critical for the next decade.

The attention cycle of issue "crises" follows a predictable pattern. There is a long period when a problem develops, largely unnoticed by the public. This is followed by the period of alarmed discovery in the media, triggered usually by some signal event: in the case of education the event was the publication of *A Nation at Risk* by the National Commission on Educational Excellence. Then, there is a flurry of intense publicity, national magazine cover stories, and major news conferences. In the next stage a few quick programs to remedy what are deep-seated and long-lasting problems are developed.

After the initial flurry of activity, the public realizes how expensive and how difficult it will be to address a fundamental problem (such as the environment) or change a basic institution (such as the schools). The next stage is a period of gradual loss of media attention and routinization of policy in terms of traditional patterns. Another problem emerges to replace the discarded issue; prison reform appears to be a good candidate for the next problem. This issue-attention cycle leads to extreme periods of interest followed by similar periods of disinterest.

Another characteristic of the issue-attention cycle is the "either/or" syndrome. During the intense period of media attention and concern, we tend to overemphasize educational objectives while underemphasizing others.[2] For example, in the late 1950s, after Sputnik, we were very concerned about the quality of education, the shortcomings of mathematics and science education, and the needs of gifted pupils. This intense activity was followed by a complete neglect of these areas as we entered the middle 1960s and became concerned with problems of cities and the disadvantaged. Now we are

---

Michael W. Kirst is professor of education, Stanford University.

seeing a cycle similar to the period in the late 1950s. Will we in turn neglect the disadvantaged and erode substantial gains we have made for the handicapped, disadvantaged, and women and other groups that gained an equal educational opportunity within the last 15 years? Part of our role as education leaders will be to provide some balance to these cycles so that we continue the equal opportunity thrust at the same time that we move forward to improve the quality of the education system. A major question is: how can we make this era more than a passing fad and take advantage of a rare opportunity to improve education?[3]

COMMON THEMES OF THE 1983 HIGH SCHOOL REPORTS

While there has been considerable attention to the various differences in the 1983 high school reports, most of them are similar in their prescriptions. Indeed, the differences are less important than the similarities. Common characteristics include:

1. The reports contend that the schools are spread over too many objectives and need to set priorities among their many potential functions, such as basic skills, improving creativity, providing vocational education, providing skills for personal development, and transmitting the common historical culture of the United States.

2. The reports contend that the high school curriculum is too fragmented, with too many electives; it is an unregulated smorgasbord.

3. The reports assert there should be more emphasis on a common core high school curriculum with particular emphasis on writing, science, mathematics, and the "higher order" skills of analysis and critical reasoning.

4. The reports contend that American school children do not do enough homework and should increase their home studies by multiples of two or three.

5. The reports advocate upgrading high school graduation requirements and college admission course requirements. Moreover, the colleges are urged to make their expectations clear about content within the required courses.

6. All the reports stress the need to attract and retain high quality teachers and to retrain the teachers we now have.

7. As a partial solution to the teacher crisis, the reports stress building career ladders for teachers so that a teacher's job description changes over time. The use of merit pay, master teachers, and built-in career steps should lead to higher social status for teachers.

8. The reports recommend increases in teacher training standards, applicable to both admission to college and certification, with more emphasis on content and subject matter rather than education methods.

9. Most reports stress the need for better training of principals so that they emphasize curriculum, leadership, and educational substance rather than administrative details. Curricular leadership should be the key to principal selection.

10. The reports call for a new partnership among schools, business, and higher education that goes beyond gimmicks, such as "adopting" a school.

11. The reports assert the primacy of states and local school districts in the delivery of education services; they mention the federal role only in a vague way.

12. The reports all have an undertone that the nation's economic prosperity depends on a higher level education for all students. We will lose our economic competitive edge to Japan and other countries if education is not improved. This link between education and economic growth has been a crucial factor in increasing media attention on education.

13. Most of the reports imply that education's promise to the public has been broken, that educators have been remiss in preparing students for college or for work. The schools have not lived up to the expectations held for them by society.

14. Lastly, the reports all mention that equality and quality must be pursued simultaneously, but equality receives much less attention.

The reports do not cover explicitly how to fund these 14 changes or how to implement them. There is very little historical context setting in the reports, which risks a repeat of past "reform" cycles that tended to overemphasize one function of the schools and to neglect others. Few ideas about what it takes to motivate pupils are provided. The reports suggest that higher standards alone will increase pupil motivation and interest.

The absence of historical context is particularly worrisome. A study of high school reform cycles from 1890 to the present indicates that during periods of conservative political movements such as 1890, 1957, and now, there has been a focus on excellence and academic standards.[4] But during periods of economic liberalism or progressive movements, such as the 1930s and the 1960s, the sole focus has been on expanding the functions of the schools and concern for disadvantaged minorities. Again, history suggests that the either/or syndrome, driven by the media issue-attention cycle, is a danger we need to watch out for.

The reports mention elementary schools but not in any substantive depth or with any clear idea as to how the elementary, middle, and high schools should work together. Most striking in its absence from the reports is any specific attention to the middle or junior high school. This area remains a relatively dark continent in terms of educational policy concern, despite the fact that such schools deal with a crucial period for forging adolescents. Student skills and motivation must be built in prior to senior high.

While these national reports deserve criticism, they have done us a great national service in highlighting many of the problems currently facing public education. If we do not make progress during the next few years in redeeming public confidence and restoring the image of quality performance, then the voucher movement and tuition tax credits will probably gain more steam. Both of these movements are in abeyance and now have very shallow political support. Federal tuition tax credits were defeated by a large congressional margin in 1984. The only movement for vouchers or tax credits is in a few states. Clearly this is an era when education is being given an opportunity to improve itself. In California business groups feel that they want to give public education a good chance for success now, but may turn to more private alternatives if they become disillusioned with current reform efforts.

Unless educators can help sustain the current positive fiscal momentum, some of the common themes of these reports will cause a trade-off mentality between the objectives and courses in the high schools. If funding increases do not exceed inflation, there will be some cutbacks in personal development areas, such as courses in jewelry making, child development, and off-campus work experience. With the current emphasis on math and science as a key ingredient for meeting economic competition, there is some danger that the humanities will receive lower priority in a reconstruction of a common core of learning activities. Consequently, humanists, particularly those concerned with art and music, must be especially vigilant that their areas are not cut out of the common core of learning.

There were some areas of disagreement among the reports. One of those was in the area of time—several groups advocated longer school days and school years. Other reports, such as those by Goodlad and Boyer, suggested that existing time within schools is wasted and could be used more efficiently through increased time on instructional tasks. The critics of the longer school day and school year stressed that it would be very expensive to make more than marginal additions to the school day; consequently, they emphasized attention to such things as minimizing class interruptions and teachers having students do their homework in class.

Only two of the reports called for a fundamental restructuring of the high school organization, those by John Goodlad and Ted Sizer. Goodlad advocated a small "house system" whereby pupils would be grouped into settings of 160 each. Sizer urges a "personalized education" including a smaller number of periods per day—perhaps as few as two. High schools would be reorganized into four large departments: Inquiry and Expression, Math and Sciences, Literature and Arts, and Philosophy and History. But even Goodlad and Sizer stop short of urging a repeal of the comprehensive high school and a focus on specialized or "magnet" schools. The report of the National Science Board mentions specialized schools in science and math, but only as an adjunct to a huge majority of comprehensive high schools. Consequently, the reports overwhelmingly emphasize doing better *within the existing structure* of secondary education rather than totally overhauling the current organizational pattern.

TENSION AND CHOICE IN THE COMPREHENSIVE HIGH SCHOOL

One way to evaluate the recommendations of these national reports is to focus on the choices that must be faced by the institution most under attack today—the comprehensive secondary school. The secondary school has built-in tensions produced by conflicts among goals and competition for resources. The national reports, with their straightforward recommendations, obscure the necessary trade-offs among goals. With limited resources, choices must be made on the following dimensions:

Governance. There is a tension between the rapid responsiveness and clear responsibility associated with a highly centralized control structure and the autonomy and flexibility associated with decentralized control systems. Most of the national reports urge more centralized academic standards at the state or local school district levels.

Professionalism. There is a tension between the desire of teachers, faced with unpredictable tasks that require discretion, to keep a high level of autonomy, and the need of governing structure to exert some pressure upon teachers in the performance of their duties. The reports move in both directions by calling for tighter central teacher evaluation programs and more attractive classroom working conditions.

Unionization. There is a tension between the power of collective instruments, like unions, in producing better working conditions or salaries for union members, and the ability of individual practitioners and governing bodies to shape the conditions of work in ways that fit task requirements. The reports do not address the benefits and costs of teacher unions.

Educational politics. There is a tension between the view of schools as part of the governmental system and subject to political decision-making either in elections or by acts of governmental officials, and the image of schools as professional bureaucracies performing highly technical tasks that are beyond the level of knowledge of the general public and its agents (school board elections versus referenda on education).

Many members of the community served by the school feel that school personnel, paid for by the community, should perform in ways that meet citizen expectations. Most educators contend that school personnel are performing tasks at a level beyond the competence of members of the general public. The reports are not explicit about who should govern public education or which of these contending views is most appropriate.

Responsiveness to subgroups within the community. There is a tension between the view of schools as serving the total community, or the typical members of the community, and the view that schools should encourage and assist the development of pluralistic cultural and social groups. The reports do not emphasize pluralism. The reports urge a common curriculum and fewer options that foster pluralistic views of what knowledge is most worth knowing.

Comprehensive versus specialized schools. There is a tension between the specialization of a school to perform a particular function, with accompanying efficiency, and the diversity and free choice available in the large comprehensive school. A few of the reports advocate magnet schools, but only as a small supplement to the comprehensive high school.

Vocational education. There is a tension between specific vocational education, usually oriented towards less qualified students, and the maintenance of a high quality program oriented towards the development of more general skills. Vocational education is not addressed in depth in most reports. The reports stress general academic skills and appear to give little priority to vocational education at the high school level.

Tracking. There is a tension between special programs (such as those for the gifted, the handicapped, bilingual pupils, and pupils in need of remedial education) requiring additional resources for students who are not capable of adequate performance in a heterogeneous pool of students, or who would not be well served participating in heterogeneous classrooms, and the maintenance of a high quality program for the remainder of the students. Some of the reports, such as Goodlad's, advocate ending tracks, but most want to stiffen the academic requirements in all tracks.

Social services. There is a tension between the school providing a variety of auxiliary functions (such as driver education) and the view of the school as having a predominantly academic mission. The reports recommend pruning the auxiliary functions and having more focus on "core academic curriculum."

TABLE 1
A Framework for Viewing Change in High Schools

(1) External Forces Establish→ Expectations, Constraints, Opportunities, Demands	(2) Time→ Dimensions	(3) Impact of (1) and (2) on→ High School	(4) Trade-Offs, Choices, Options
• Ideology is muddled.	• Past	• Functions	• Spell out the options, show the trade-offs.
• Political forces conflict and no one is clearly in charge.		• Pupil Outcomes	
		• Design	
• Demography enrollment shrinks but then rises after 1990.	• Current	• Structure	
• Fiscal interacts with ideology and demography.	• Future	• Specifically, Governance, Vocational Education, Tracking, Social Services, Citizenship, Broad Competencies, Diversity of Offerings, College Preparatory	

Citizenship or jobs. There is a tension between the school socializing youths to perform their duties as adult citizens and the view that the primary mission of the school is to prepare youths for their future occupations. The reports stress citizenship and academic learning with less time devoted to preparation for specific jobs.

Diversity of offerings. There is a tension between the provision of numerous course alternatives and choices for students, and the investment of resources in producing a higher quality but more limited core program. Again, choice is downplayed and viewed as undesirable.

Preparatory education. Finally, there is a tension between the secondary school viewed as the end of education for a large number of its students and the view that the secondary school should articulate with and prepare for the types of postsecondary education that are available in the community.

A framework for rethinking American education policy that relates the changing external context in the first part of the paper to the tension and choices in the second is presented in Table 1. Several external forces such as demography and fiscal constraints change over time. These external forces are filtered through a particular context now and in the future. These changing and conflicting forces have an impact on specific functions, programs, and organizational factors in secondary education. The result is the tension and necessity for trade-offs that are discussed above.

FINANCING REFORM

The 1984 fiscal outlook for the states is for short-term improvement because of the economic recovery and this year's tax increases. In the longer term, fiscal problems are likely to continue unless the national economy is embarked on a sustained period of robust growth—which is doubtful. Besides the economy, factors determining the fiscal prospects of states and localities are federal aid (a negative) and taxpayer attitudes.

TABLE 2
Approaches to Educational Equity and Excellence

	Education Excellence	School Finance Equity
Goals:	Education quality	Fiscal equity
Focus:	Education processes	Education programs
	Use of dollars	Level of dollars
	The gifted and talented, mathematics and science, and average student	The low achiever, poor, and handicapped student
Mechanisms:	Competitive grants	Formula grants
	Differentiate by quality	Differentiate by wealth
	Rewards school improvement	Reimburses for costs
Impact and Style:	Tends to integrate for education improvement	Tends to fragment for fiscal tracking
	Targeted aid, some districts to get no aid	General aid, all districts get some aid
	Technical assistance oriented	Compliance oriented
	Lower cost	Higher cost

Source: Allan Odden, Educational Commission of the States, 1983.

State officials gambled in 1983 that citizens would support tax increases. Factors contributing to a favorable climate for tax increases included the federal tax cuts, federal aid reductions, earlier state tax cuts, and well publicized state austerity measures. Tax protestors were nevertheless waiting to pounce on the states for having the temerity to raise taxes, and 1984 will be a major year for tax revolt battles. Ballot initiatives are expected in Oregon, Florida, California, Massachusetts, Michigan, and other states. Some of these measures would produce very significant tax reductions including "Jarvis IV" in California.

In numerous polls the public has indicated that it would pay more for improved education quality. The economic trends appear to be favorable and might provide more flexibility in state and local tax yields. New leadership has emerged from business and government organized around the link between education and economic growth. The prognosis for education funding has shifted from steady state (no real growth but keeping up with inflation) to cautious optimism around slow but steady improvement.[5] Many states will provide significant increases in school aid in 1985. Tax increases earmarked formally or informally for education are much easier to pass than other tax increases. Currently, education is politically popular, but it will face greater future competition for funds from social programs due to federal cutbacks.

This may finance reform by addition—more math courses, merit pay on top of base pay—rather than low-cost reallocations. Low-cost school improvement strategies may continue, but in some states like California and Florida, big new money infusions have been linked to the high school reform agenda summarized in the first section. It has been estimated that raising teacher salaries by $10,000 will cost over $20 billion. Extending the school day by 20 percent will cost another $20 billion. These are huge increases. Clearly, the search for low-cost improvement strategies should be intensified. The expanded state funds in 1984 probably will not be sufficient to eliminate the necessity for trade-offs and difficult choices highlighted in the preceding section.

The major school finance movement in the 1970s focused on equitable distribution and property tax reform. The new movement for excellence in California and Florida, for example, has distributed new program dollars without regard to districts' needs or ability to pay. Such "innovations" as mentor teachers, curriculum improvement, and longer school days are completely reimbursed by the state with wealthy school districts receiving the same amount as poor ones. This puts excellence on a collision course with equity. This emerging problem needs to be reconciled soon in order to forestall court suits and unnecessary conflict. Reformers must be careful that debates over excellence or quality are sensitive to the needs of minorities, pupils with special needs, and low wealth school districts. The differences in the approaches to educational equity and excellence are outlined in Table 2.

The state reforms of 1983–1985 pose a new challenge for calculating "appropriate" costs. For instance, how much should a core curriculum, mentor teacher, or additional writing teachers cost? If more homework presumably costs nothing additional, what about a graduation requirement of two years of science? In California, 80 separate reforms were put in SB 813, but the costs were estimated and paid mostly in a lump sum for general unrestricted aid.

The major concern about teacher quality also raises novel finance issues. States like California and Florida are throwing out a whole set of "lures" for attracting and retaining teachers. What is the cost-effectiveness of loan forgiveness, scholarships, a higher minimum salary, mentor teaching positions, and merit pay? Which of these concepts provides the most teacher retention for any fixed cost? No one has the answers. We are clearly at the experimental stage or "the cutting edge of ignorance" about what types and amounts of incentives receive the best response by prospective and current teachers. State policy is now moving in contradictory directions. On the one hand, there are more state tests and explicit curricular standards that will discourage many people from entering teaching. Numerous teachers desire autonomy and the ability to adapt the curriculum to their own style and diverse pupil needs. On the other hand, states are developing career ladders and pay scales to lure more talented people into teaching.

The current reform agenda implies that school finance will be stressing "micro" issues rather than the "macro" or equitable distribution issues of the 1970s. Higher standards, increased learning time, stricter discipline, and teacher compensation are some of the legislative remedies. More school finance research will go into the schoolhouse and the classroom and less attention will be devoted to distribution formulas. School finance research will penetrate the "technical core" of teaching, curriculum, and classroom settings. Cost-effectiveness will receive more emphasis, and evaluation of categorical programs, such as bilingual education, will receive less. This calls for a new alliance among curriculum, teacher education, and school finance researchers. There are so many reforms in states like California and Florida that there must be powerful interaction effects. The states that have funded new reforms, however, have tended to back into the needed dollars from available revenue. The state reform packages have been omnibus bills rather than the discrete, relatively focussed programs of the 1960s and 1970s.

CONCLUSION

American public education has a new agenda, new momentum, and a strong rationale (the link between education and economic growth) for major policy change. There will be a relatively brief period when education is in the spotlight as a national issue. The role of education leaders is to move expeditiously, but with a balanced agenda that does not repeat the mistakes of the past. It is imperative that educators take advantage of the favorable external context. This paper stresses that difficult choices will need to be made despite this favorable climate. A key guideline should be to pursue this new agenda in a balanced fashion that does not succumb to the excesses of past issue-attention cycles.

The new state reforms enacted in the 1983–84 legislative sessions embody broad multiple targets that seek to alter simultaneously many components of school operations. Some of the reforms include:[6]

- Tougher high school graduation requirements in 35 states. In California, where requirements had been left to local districts, a new law requires 13 credits—one credit equals one year of course work—for graduation. By 1986, Florida will require 24 units for graduation—up from 18—including three years of math and science.
- Revised textbooks and curricula in 21 states. In Texas, textbook selection methods now allow for more discussion and better books.
- Improved teacher training and certification programs in 18 states. Arkansas teachers must take a basic skills test when they renew teaching certificates.
- Longer school days and school years in 16 states. North Carolina is entering the second year of a pilot program lengthening the school year from 180 days to 200 days.

Even more changes are ahead: Maine, Illinois, and Oklahoma have education studies under way. Most plans call for more funding, especially for higher teacher salaries.

Several states boosted school aid in 1984. They are: Tennessee ($350 million), New York ($500 million), Alaska ($20 million), Texas ($2.8 billion over three years), Arkansas ($148 million), and California ($2.1 billion).

These reforms lack programmatic connections that create a specific "program" like compensatory or vocational education. This implies a set of actions that will take various forms at the local level under the rubric of "higher standards" or "excellence." This new agenda will change policy research and evaluation. New indicators of school system response will need to be developed.

State policymakers have taken the first steps toward improving the education system. After the governors and legislatures have had their say, it will be up to local school boards and school administrators to implement new curricula, new teacher pay systems, and new ways to evaluate effectiveness.

NOTES

1. Among these reports are: National Commission on Excellence in Education, *A Nation at Risk* (Washington, D.C.: U.S. Government Printing Office, 1983); Mortimer J. Adler, *The Paideia Proposal* (New York: Macmillan, 1982); John I. Goodlad, *A Place Called School: Prospects for the Future* (New York: McGraw-Hill, 1983); Twentieth Century Fund Task Force on Federal Elementary and Secondary Education Policy, *Making the Grade* (New York: Twentieth Century Fund, 1983); Ernest L. Boyer, *High Schools* (New York: Harper & Row, 1983); College Board Educational Equality Project, *Academic Preparation for College: What Students Need to Know and Be Able to Do* (New York: College Board, 1983); Theodore R. Sizer, *Horace's Compromise: The Dilemma of the American High School* (Boston: Houghton Mifflin, 1984); Task Force on Education for Economic Growth, *Action for Excellence* (Denver: Educational Commission of the States, 1983); and National Science Board Commission on Precollege Education in Mathematics, Science, and Technology, *Educating Americans for the 21st Century* (Washington, D.C.: U.S. Government Printing Office, 1983).
2. Harold Howe II, "Education Moves to Center Stage: An Overview of Recent Studies," *Phi Delta Kappan* (November 1983), p. 168.
3. Paul Peterson, "Did the Education Commissions Say Anything?" *Brookings Review* 2 (1983), p. 4.
4. Thomas James and David Tyack, "Learning from Past Efforts to Reform the High School," *Phi Delta Kappan* (February 1983), pp. 400–406.
5. See Michael W. Kirst and Walter I. Garms, "The Political Environment of School Finance Policy in the 1980s," in James Guthrie, ed., *School Finance Policy and Practices* (Cambridge: Ballinger, 1980), pp. 47–48.
6. *USA Today*, July 27, 1984.

CHARLES S. BENSON

State Government Contributions to the Public Schools

In 1979–80, state government for the first time became the primary supplier of revenue to support and maintain public elementary and secondary schools, displacing by a slight margin the contributions of local school districts themselves. (See Steven Gold's paper for the exact figures.) The dollar amount of state aid for local schools in 1980–81 was $50.2 billion. This sum represented 21 percent of state revenue from own sources; it was approximately equal to the amount that state governments spent on public welfare in 1981 and twice what they spent on highways.[1]

At the end of World War I, local authorities were contributing 83.2 percent of the money for schools and the state contribution was only 16.5 percent. What conditions account for the increase in the state share? Major increases in state contributions have occurred in three decades only: the 1930s, the 1940s, and the 1970s.

In the 1930s a number of local school districts were in serious financial trouble because their local property tax bases became eroded by the depression. To stave off fiscal collapse, state governments stepped in. The larger state role was also in part a political phenomenon. Parents joined forces with teachers to put pressure on state legislatures to accept responsibility to improve the schools, stressing the argument that only state government had both the means and the obligation to make the availability of educational resources more equal among various school districts and to create an opportunity for all willing youth to receive a secondary education. This political force was greatly assisted by faculty in education departments of universities, especially the faculty of Teachers College.[2] The upshot was that the state share rose from 16.9 percent in 1929–30 to 30.3 percent in 1939–40.

The next big jump, up to a state share of 39.8 percent, took place in the second half of the decade of the 1940s. These were years when school facilities were being expanded rapidly to accommodate children of the World War II baby boom and to facilitate the suburbanization of the white middle-class family. From 1947–48 until 1971–72, the state share remained within the range of 37.4 percent to 39.8 percent. This means that the relative size of the state share did not change as a result of the post-Sputnik effort to improve instruction in mathematics and science or as a result of

---

Charles S. Benson is a professor in the Department of Education at the University of California, Berkeley.

the attempt of President Johnson to use elementary/secondary education as a major instrument in his war on poverty.

In 1973–74 state contributions to education, relative to local and federal shares, began to rise again. This rise during the 1970s appears to have been related mainly to two conditions: (1) the taxpayer revolt, which considerably limited local governments' access to the property tax base in a number of states and (2) school finance reform, stimulated at least in part by judicial intervention.[3]

THE OBJECTIVES OF STATE GOVERNMENT IN ASSISTING LOCAL SCHOOL DISTRICTS

The states have a number of objectives in providing aid to school districts: (1) to assure that education services are adequate; (2) to promote local control; (3) to stabilize revenue flows; and (4) to eradicate disparities in expenditures and tax burdens, otherwise known as "equalization."

Adequacy of Provision

Even if frontier America had no great longing or respect for classical studies, the people of our country attribute importance to plain learning, or the basic skills of communication. The notion is deeply inbred that democracy would be a risky venture without an educated electorate. We have established an imperative for a broad-based system of education. Thus, from the beginning of settlement in America, the idea was accepted that the public must contribute toward the cost of providing education and that education carries social value exceeding the sum of the educational benefits to individual families.

It was a rather easy step, then, to say just as the taxpayer of a community helped families to educate their children, the larger community of the state should help local school districts pay for their schools.

Early interventions by the states were modest in scope and designed to expand enrollment. Toward this end, they took the simple form of flat grants, or a given sum of dollars for each enrolled pupil. Expansions and a concern with the quality of instruction were joined in the proposals of Ellwood Cubberly (1906); Cubberly wanted the states to pay money to school districts to meet a portion of teachers' salaries, and he was widely influential.[4] By the mid-1920s Professors Strayer and Haig of Columbia University launched an idea that proved to be extremely popular with policymakers. They proposed that the state set a dollar floor, a minimum expenditure level, for each pupil and, further, that the state assure each district the means to meet the minimum level of expenditure at a reasonable local tax rate, after taking the state's contribution into account. Strayer and Haig advocated that states establish a "foundation program plan" to accomplish their objectives; it is still the most widely used fiscal device in elementary/secondary education.

Expansion of an educational system to serve all of the children of a state is, in a democracy, one concept of adequacy. Since the Strayer-Haig formula paid out money to local authorities on the basis of the number of pupils, it retained an incentive to expand the count of students served. However, by the 1930s reasonably effective enforcement of compulsory attendance laws allowed the concern for adequacy to shift from expansion *per se* to the quality of education services. During the 1930s, 1940s, and 1950s, educators sought to impress state legislators with the idea that better education was needed and that better education called for more money than the local authorities were willing to spend. Teachers, parents, administrators, and university faculty tried to advance this idea without talking much about the results, or outcomes, of schooling. Current ideas about adequacy place a great deal of emphasis on results. We want the schools to provide an early understanding of mathematics and science so that graduates, after further work at M.I.T. or Cal Tech, become brilliant inventors who protect our economy from foreign competition. Alternatively, we want our middle school students to be as good or better at mathematics as Japanese students. Or we want the schools to train children from low-income families in basic skills and good work habits, so that they become employed and not a public burden. Or we want the schools to inculcate ideas about the sanctity of the family and about being unselfish, so that we have fewer broken homes. Or all of the above, plus more.

From the point of view of state government, there are two great difficulties in linking ideas of adequacy and accountability for results. The first difficulty is that we don't know very well how to accomplish defined objectives in schools; hence, we don't know how much the different objectives cost or how much state aid is needed.[5] The second main difficulty is the ideology of local control.

Maintenance of Local Control

From the beginnings of our country, most of our educational leaders have been distrustful of giving powers of control over our schools to higher levels of government. The force of localism remains strong. Whether still grounded in the philosophy of John Stuart Mill or in a more pragmatic concern of middle-class children, localism is a superb adaptation to political reality in a pluralistic, capitalistic society.

In addition, local control is assumed to offer substantive advantages for education. People are thought to be more willing to pay taxes for education if they have a large voice in how the money is spent, and they are ordinarily concerned to exercise a voice in the affairs of schools closest to them. Localism contributes to a vitality of parental involvement in schools and to an exploration of alternative instructional methods. It fosters a healthy competition to raise standards of achievement. It strengthens community identity, especially by means of school athletics. Following the Tiebout hypothesis, it allows families of strong, conservative educational tastes and wealth to establish exclusive, quasi-private schools while retaining the benefit of IRS deductions for their local property taxes.[6]

All these points behoove state legislators and state departments of education to move cautiously in restricting powers of local school districts. Not that encroachment doesn't occur. The state education codes of such large states as New York and California are prolix in the extreme. States generally are involved in setting policies in the following areas: length of school year, length of school day, processes for teacher certification, tenure of certificated teachers, teacher dismissal procedures, qualifications of administrators, nature of teacher salary schedules, treatment of handicapped children, procedures for testing, scope of bargaining, minimum curricula, and requirements for a high school diploma.

What do state governments refrain from doing in the name of maintaining control of education? First, they do not take direct action to redraw district boundaries. Second, they do not set limits on what kinds of educational services can be provided. Third, they make no attempt to regulate state grants to localities by criteria of efficiency, meaning that well-managed districts receive no reward and badly-managed districts receive no penalty. Fourth, they do not seek to control the assignment of particular teachers to particular schools. Fifth, states eschew detailed regulation of local district budgets. This last point means that the largest portion of state funds distributed to school districts by states is in the form of ''general purpose'' (or block) grants, meaning unrestricted as to use by school districts, subject to the generalized state mandates of the types listed above.

This ''hands off the local budget'' approach has created a curious dilemma. Since 1965 a strong attempt has been made to cause state distributions to be more sensitive to the educational requirements of different types of pupils. States have been urged to provide extra money for students in kindergarten through grade 3; for vocational pupils, differentiated by speciality; for several categories of handicapped pupils; for bilingual pupils; for economically disadvantaged pupils; and for gifted (just to name the most common categories). Under the argument that equal treatment of unequals is both unjust and inefficient, grant differentiation by student category makes sense.

One way to accomplish such differentiation is to use categorical grants, funds intended to be used for particular services. This procedure runs afoul of the general preference of state government to use block grants for schools. Alternatively, one may assign expenditure weights to different types of pupils under the main, general purpose grant: a disadvantaged pupil is weighted at 1.5, a gifted student at 1.65, and so on to reflect the additional cost, relative to a ''regular'' pupil, of serving the pupil with special, high-cost needs. This method is growing in popularity and it may appear to solve the problem, but it doesn't. If the state government monitors the use of the weighted funds closely, perhaps even requiring local matching, then it involves itself in detailed control of local budgets, an act implicitly forbidden. If the state government doesn't monitor the weighted expenditures, it provides an almost irresistible temptation to local authorities to make a profit on the extra funds they receive for the special pupils; that is, districts divert the funds to the benefit of regular students and their teachers. Profit-making in turn leads to mislabeling, or over-labeling, of students. When low-income and minority students are mislabeled into categories of mildly handicapped or educationally retarded, the damage to these children can be serious. Thus, the objective of developing a more sophisticated, educationally realistic, and cost-conscious system of state grants for education and the objective of maintaining a high degree of local control are not thoroughly compatible.

Stability in Revenue Flows

School districts spend most of their budgets on items that are fixed in the short term. Service on long-term debt is one example but much bigger in amount is the sum paid out for teachers' salaries. Most teachers are tenured employees and it would be regarded as unconscionable for a state government to force a given school district to fire teachers that hold tenure as defined by state law.

Furthermore, useful, constructive change at the local level often requires district administrators to make middle-term commitments to new types of teaching staff. If local administrators thought their entitlement to state funds was highly volatile from one year to the next, they would be stifled in their attempts to be innovative about program design and instructional procedures. This program becomes more serious as the share of school support provided by state government becomes larger.

Accordingly, when a state government contemplates a major change in its school aid formulas, it looks carefully to see which districts would lose money. These affected districts may have the power to block the change, almost always called a "reform," in the legislature. It is common practice to buy them off, and there are two chief methods. One is to phase in the change in grant arrangements over a period of years. The other is a grandfather clause, to "hold harmless" districts that might stand to lose money. A number of states have become notorious for their use of hold-harmless provisions.

A second concern of state government in providing a stable source of revenue is in the matter of choice of formula. Those formulas are preferred that imply a long-term commitment of funds by the state. A formula cannot be open-ended, committing the state to unlimited spending; rather, it should generally define the state's obligation. Nevertheless, it is not uncommon to find that a state legislature fails to provide an annual appropriation large enough to fund its school formula fully.

Eradication of Disparities in Expenditures and Local Tax Burdens: Equalization

Most state governments place considerable emphasis on reducing disparities in expenditures per pupil and in local school tax rates. Two different arguments apply, one for expenditures and one for tax rates.

Regarding expenditures, the idea is that all rational variations in expenditure per pupil are tied to some educational condition, such as learning requirements of pupils or the relative power of a given district in the market for teachers' services or some other condition that affects the true costs of providing educational services. In fact, one can observe a relationship in most states between local taxable values per pupil and expenditures per pupil. Property values are commonly thought to be unrelated to educational conditions, so efforts are made to reduce the relationship between expenditures and taxable values. If nothing else is done at the same time, this type of "reform" can be very harmful to big city districts.

Likewise, it is commonly held that household income should not be a dominant factor in determining educational expenditures. Insofar as expenditure differentials account for educational outcomes, giving the children of rich parents advantages in public schools, beyond those they have at home, is regarded as bad policy on two counts. It lessens the amount of true meritocracy in our society, and it perpetuates hereditary class distinctions. Unfairness to children is ordinarily held to be a more serious sin than unfairness to adults, who are in part responsible themselves for their conditions. But there is a second reason. Insofar as public school policy favors rich children, some rich children will be pushed ahead beyond their natural capacities and some poor children of considerable talent will fail to get the training and jobs appropriate to their natural gifts. Overall, the result is a waste of known talent in our society.

Some state courts have thus taken the position that the only sure way to eradicate the influence of taxable wealth and household income on school expenditures is to demand equality of expenditures per student. Most people in the school finance community disagree. There are concentrations of hard-to-educate youth in certain types of school districts and this fact should be recognized by providing such districts with extra funds.

There are also differential cost conditions among districts. Regarding the major condition of variation, the cost of teachers' services, Alan L. Gustman and M.O. Clement have written:

> [Our] findings imply that inter-area differences in the supply price of teachers' services constitute an independent force that has caused some inequality of education. . . . Equality of educational expenditures between areas need not mean that students are receiving equal amounts of real resources: unequal expenditures are not necessarily a sign of inequality . . . given the importance of supply price in determining teachers' salaries, there is no hope that those current school and property tax reforms that are designed to equalize purchasing power among districts in *dollar* terms will eliminate educational problems created by inter-area differences in factor price.[7]

Differences in supply price of teachers' services are caused primarily by teachers' preferences regarding where they want to live and whom they want to teach. A district located in an industrial ghetto with a record of police brutality and with dirty air would probably have to pay more to obtain a highly competent teacher than an upper-class community in a pleasant site known for its cultural amenities.

Some states appear to take the position that they have fulfilled their obligation to education if all children are taught under conditions that meet a minimum standard. Minimum standards are commonly described in terms of a class size, the presence of a certified teacher, and the availability of a standard set of instructional materials. Organized teachers are more likely to take the position that disparities must be judged relatively and that when disparities in a state become wide, as between the highest and lowest spending districts, the state is obligated to increase the amount of aid it distributes to school districts. Because of their staked claim to this argument, teachers are generally opposed to policies that put a lid on the expenditures of high spending districts.

With regard to disparities in local tax rates, the argument for reducing extreme variations has to do with the likelihood that the variations will become capitalized in land value, with the results that consumer choice of households in the public sector *a la* Tiebout becomes restricted and industry becomes overly concentrated in tax havens. Another argument suggests that tax rate differences need not be eliminated but set in a positive, monotonic relationship to school expenditures per student, essentially a proposition in horizontal equity.

To conclude this section, it should be noted that some objectives do not guide the distribution of state grants for education in any serious degree:

- Cost-effective operation of school districts.
- Meeting requirements of the labor market for trained workers.
- Maximization of student achievement subject to a budget constraint.
- Reduction or elimination of the achievement gap associated with socioeconomic status.
- Redrawing district boundaries to reduce segregation by socioeconomic status.
- Reduction of intradistrict resource disparities.

States ordinarily do not use financial incentives to accomplish the above.

THE MAIN FISCAL DEVICES OF EDUCATIONAL FINANCE

States usually distribute funds to support the current operating expenses of school districts through the use of a formula. Most states have so many districts that case-by-case negotiation of state aid would be unmanageable. Approximately 85 percent of state money for schools is distributed under such formulas. All of the formulas in use contain some element to indicate need-to-spend and all contain some element to describe local taxable wealth. The main idea is to distribute the state's money directly in relation to need-to-spend and inversely with respect to local wealth. Nevertheless, we can classify formulas in terms of whether they are primarily need-based or primarily aimed at tax base equalization.

Need-Based Formulas

The prototype is the foundation program plan, also called the Strayer-Haig formula or a fixed-unit equalization plan. The entitlement of a district is the positive difference between an estimate made by the state of need to spend and an estimate, again made by the state, of a fair local contribution toward that objective. In simplest form the formula is:

$$A_i = N_i u - rY_i,$$

where A_i = state grant to the ith district; N_i = count of students in the ith district; Y_i = local tax base in the ith district; u = dollar value of the "foundation program," a sum of money intended to show what it would cost to provide a typical student in a typical district with an adequate education; and r = a computational tax rate, intended to establish a fair local contribution to public schools.

In setting values for u and r, states obviously take account of the condition of the state's budget and the public mood toward tax increases. The value of u is ordinarily set near the state average expenditure. The early advocates of this fiscal device suggested that r should be set to provide no state aid to the state's richest district. This would mean that all districts in the state could provide their students with the foundation program at no higher tax rate than the richest district paid.

This is one criterion of efficiency, but no state has accepted such a pure form of the grant. Assuming that the foundation program is priced realistically, such a low rate of local contribution—rich districts ordinarily are very rich—would establish a very expensive grant program. To accommodate the foundation program formula to the state budget requires the local contribution rate to be raised to a fairly high level. This means the formula is rather weak in eliminating disparities in expenditures and tax rates, especially when a state follows the common practice of giving every district a minimum flat grant per student regardless of local wealth. Generally, the upshot is that poorer districts have low expenditures per student and high tax rates, with opposite conditions prevailing in rich districts.

It is now common practice to provide that the foundation program be subject to price-level escalation; otherwise, the aggregate of state aid will be squeezed down by the inflationary rise in taxable values. It is also becoming more common to use various kinds of pupil weightings in the formula.

It is easy to imagine a need-based formula that would yield a lot more equalization for the state dollar. For example, consider the following: (1) determine a statewide average school tax rate; (2) apply that rate to the tax base of each district and divide by the number of pupils in each district. Call that dollar sum the relative financial ability of each district (RFA); (3) rank all districts in RFA, highest to lowest; and (4) begin distributing state educational money to the poorest district and bring it up in spending power to the RFA of the second poorest; bring those two districts up to the RFA of the third poorest, etc., and continue the process until the state's education money is exhausted. This is essentially the procedure used in New Hampshire to pay out general purpose money for schools.

Tax Base Equalization

There are several closely-related forms of tax base equalization. One form is percentage equalization, using the formula:

$$A_i = N_i[(1 - x \cdot \frac{y_i}{\bar{y}}) e_i]$$

where A_i = state grant to the ith district; N_i = count of students; x = arbitrary constant, ($0 < x = 1$); y_i = assessed property value per student in the ith district; y = statewide average assessed valuation; and e_i = state-local expenditure per student.

The formula requires the state to share in a locally determined education budget, with the state assuming a higher share in poor districts than rich ones. Oftentimes, both an upper and lower level of expenditure is stated. The lower limit is a mandatory floor, but the upper is not necessarily a ceiling—more commonly, it is the point beyond which the state will not share in an expenditure increase. Sometimes the rate of state sharing is less at high expenditure levels than at low. This is called putting a "kink" in the schedule; it is intended to offer extra stimulation to low-spending districts while at the same time curbing profligacy.

The only variable for the state to set in such a formula is x, and x represents approximately the total local share of educational spending (excluding federal money). Thus, if x is 0.4, the state assumes approximately 60 percent of the aggregate state-local budget.

If the formula is fully operational, it will provide the following result: any two school districts that levy the same local tax rate will have equal expenditures per student. This is another criterion of equity. However, in most states, to get this result requires that rich districts receive negative aid, meaning that the rich districts turn over part of their local tax receipts to the state for redistribution. (Alternatively, the state could assume a very high share of the total educational budget.) Negative aid has not found favor in many states (although Montana and Wyoming use such an approach). That fact, combined with the practice of giving every district some minimum grant, means that percentage grants are seldom very equalizing.

"Power equalizing" and "guaranteed yield" formulas are alternative versions of the percentage equalizing scheme. In all three forms it is growing practice to use a count of weighted students.

The percentage sharing approach has been popular in New England and from time to time in New York. It was adopted by the California legislature in 1977 but was knocked out by the passage of Proposition 13. Several states use a combination of the foundation program formula and percentage equalizing with the sharing formula resting on top of the foundation program base.

Refining the Fiscal Instruments.

States do not simply adopt one of the formulas described in the last section and let it go at that. The states attempt considerable refinements, adding greatly to the complexity of the distributions.

One approach is the use of categorical grants that are separate from general aid. Categorical grants are typically used to provide state aid for school construction or transportation. The state either supports an equalized share of local costs or reimburses districts at a state-determined cost rate per pupil. Alternatively, the state may pay a portion of the excess cost of providing particular services.

Lately, much interest has been given to shifting or rolling up the categorical grants into the main distribution formula for general aid. This can be done by using weighted pupils. Florida was one of the first states to place heavy emphasis on this procedure. In 1974 that state adopted a new general aid scheme that included weights for several types of handicapped pupils, for gifted pupils, and for six categories of vocational pupils.[8] Currently, Utah uses 21 weights to recognize the extra costs of operating small schools at the elementary, junior high, senior high, and six-year school levels. There are 16 types of weightings for handicapped children and six for vocational education. The state also uses a staff cost factor to take account of differences among districts in the training and experience of teachers.[9]

How are the weights determined? In earlier times it was common practice to rely upon the opinion of experts. Now, weights are most often arrived at by expenditure analysis. Neither approach is entirely adequate. The experts are likely to be advocates for the particular programs they are costing and their weights may be overly generous. Expenditure analysis tends to rely upon existing data and rules-of-thumb to make pro-rations of teacher time and instructional space. The process of prorating expenditures is difficult when the client population is "mainstreamed" (taught in classrooms with normal children). Expenditure analysis seldom takes account of the fact that districts may contain significant numbers of eligible but undiscovered clients for given programs.[10]

Another type of refinement that is now being introduced in state aid distributions is a cost-of-education index. Here, Florida and Missouri lead the way. The main intent of using an index is to compensate districts that have a disadvantage in the market for teachers' services. While Florida uses a cost-of-living approach, Missouri uses an econometric approach that attempts to separate variables under the control of school districts from those not under their control.[11]

The intent is to confine cost-of-education index values to relative differences in the strength of supply variables, leaving aside the matter of the relative strength of the demand variables. The index, that is, is not intended to reward districts that pay teachers a lot of money solely for the reason that inhabitants of those districts have a high preference for educational services.

Yet another refinement has not gone far beyond the discussion stages—namely, the proposal to confine local taxation for education to residential properties, leaving industrial and commercial properties to be taxed for education on a statewide basis. The intent is to bring local taxable wealth more closely in line with household income. Instead, nine states have chosen to incorporate household income directly into their formulas.[12]

All of these refinements tend to create complexity in state aid distributions, and the complexity renders them beyond the patience of the average citizen to understand. In New York, state aid for education is paid out under 20 separate formulas. Most of these are categorical in nature, but the total amount of categorical aid in New York in 1982–83 amounted to only 2.4 percent of state support of elementary and secondary education.[13] In California the combination of the legal imperative to equalize expenditures and Proposition 13 has led the state to take over educational financing completely. Even though some property tax revenue is used to support schools, school districts have no discretion regarding property tax rates nor do they benefit or suffer as the property tax base per pupil goes up or down. Lacking the power to balance their budgets with local revenue, the districts look to Sacramento to take care of them in their widely differing circumstances. This puts great pressure on the state to make very precise adjustments in state distributions for education, and part of the California education code that deals with finance is beginning to look like the federal Internal Revenue Code. California districts now hire consultants to help them fill out their state aid forms just as households and businesses hire tax accountants to help them fill out their federal tax returns.

STATE AID DISTRIBUTIONS AND LOCAL INCENTIVES

What incentives do state aid programs create for local districts?

Maintenance of pupil enrollment. The strongest incentive is to maintain pupil enrollment. In most parts of the country, state aid is a significant source of school revenue. Most states distribute their assistance on the basis of a count of pupils, as modified by equalization, weighting, etc. If a district loses pupils, it suffers a loss of state aid. It will probably find it hard to offset that loss with an increase in local revenues, and it will almost certainly find it very hard to balance its budget, given that so many of its expenditures are made under long-term controls.

Districts fear two kinds of pupil desertion: entry into private schools and the movement of families with children out of the district. (Losses for demographic reasons are not feared so much, because that problem is shared with other districts and the state government is likely to adopt a statewide palliative.) The first fear reinforces the opposition of educators to vouchers and tax credits, these being seen as devices to encourage private education. The second fear leads school administrators to be cautious: not to argue for desegregation, to be middle-of-the-road in politics, not to favor any special groups of pupils, except perhaps those bound for elite colleges, not to examine teacher assignment practices very closely, etc. Fear of loss of enrollment also leads most districts to oppose interdistrict sharing of pupils, even when it is demonstrably to the advantage of certain pupils.

To identify or not to identify. The existence of grants that are categorical by type of pupil and the use of weightings raise the question at the district level as to whether it is worthwhile to identify pupils with special needs and gifts. One may assume that both overidentification and underidentification are bad. If the extra funds earned for the district by some special kind of pupil exceed the cost of serving those pupils in the local district or if it is expected that the uses of the special funds will not be monitored, then an incentive for overidentification may exist. Opposite conditions may produce an incentive for underidentification, i.e., overlooking special problems and gifts. The incentives for over and underidentification may be different for different types of districts, i.e., they may not be uniform over the whole state.

District size. In most states there are special allocations for small districts having to do with personnel costs and pupil transport costs. In sparsely populated areas, these allocations make good sense, but not all small districts are found in such places; they exist as well in metropolitan areas. The corrections for size may encourage districts that are unnecessarily small to remain small, thus perpetuating inefficiency.

District budgets. In states where a major portion of state assistance is distributed under some kind of percentage sharing scheme, there may be an incentive for rich school districts to shift parts of their budgets into the municipal budget. Libraries and recreation functions would be likely targets, especially if the net local cost of providing the service in the school budget is higher than the net local cost in the municipality.

OUTLOOK FOR THE FUTURE.

Predictions are always hazardous but here are mine for state financing of education during the 1980s:

- States will seek to shift resources, in the relative sense, into college preparatory programs and away from other instructional programs at the secondary level.
- States will increase the pressure on local districts for academic performance of pupils.
- States will display less tolerance for academic and cultural diversity than they did in the 1960s and 1970s.

To accomplish these goals, states will modify their aid programs (1) to offer financial rewards to districts that show increases in pupil achievement, and (2) to offer financial rewards to districts that adopt differentiated salary schedules. These changes will not reduce the complexity of the state grant systems and may in fact increase it. That the changes may represent further encroachment on local control will not be seen as a matter of great concern in state legislatures.

Lastly, I expect that states will give a lot more attention than they have in the past to teacher training and teacher certification. Education is still the easiest so-called profession to enter, and it has attracted more than its share of people who are unable to perform well. Worse than that, pedagogical skill is not demanded of new teachers in the general case, nor are intending teachers well instructed in the diagnosis of and prescription for learning problems of individual students. To bring into the teaching profession persons who know well their subjects to teach, and who are up-to-date in the growing field of knowledge of how students learn at different stages of their mental development, is both the greatest challenge and biggest opportunity that the states face in education. Thus, educational progress may come not so much from a manipulation of state cash grants for schools as from better administration and leadership in subsidization of teacher training and certification. The strategic element of state involvement, accordingly, is likely to be this form of aid-in-kind.

NOTES

1. Bureau of the Census, *Statistical Abstract of the United States: 1984* (Washington, D.C.: Government Printing Office, 1984), pp. 275, 289.
2. Billy D. Walker, "The Local Property Tax for Public Schools: Some Historical Perspectives," *Journal of Education Finance* 9 (Winter 1984), pp. 286–287.
3. Lawrence L. Brown, Alan L. Ginsburg, J. Neil Killalea, Richard A. Rosthall, and Esther O. Tron, "School Finance Reform in the Seventies: Achievements and Failures," *Journal of Education Finance* 4 (Fall 1978), pp. 210–211.

4. Charles S. Benson, *The Economics of Public Education* (Boston, Mass.: Houghton Mifflin Co., 1961), pp. 195–201.
5. I would say that the main event to link ideas of adequacy and quantitative educational results was the passage of the Elementary and Secondary Act of 1965. It stressed improvement in achievement of low-income children and the reporting of results by districts to states and by states to the federal government. It is surely no coincidence that the early attempts to describe an educational production function by regression analysis date from that very year.
6. Thomas W. Vitullo-Martin, "The Impact of Taxation Policy on Public and Private Schools" in Robert B. Everhart, ed., *The Public School Monopoly: A Critical Analysis of Education and the State in American Society* (Cambridge: Ballinger Publishing Company, 1982).
7. Alan L. Gustman and M.O. Clement, "Teachers' Salary Differentials and Equality of Educational Opportunity," *Industrial and Labor Relations Review* 31 (October 1977), p. 70.
8. Governor's Citizen's Committee on Education, *Improving Education in Florida* (Tallahassee, Fla.: Committee on Education, 1973).
9. F. Heber Fuller, "Cost Differentials: Utah's New School Finance Formula," *Journal of Education Finance* 1 (Winter 1976), pp. 373–378.
10. J.S. Kakalik, W.S. Furry, M.A. Thomas, and M.F. Carney, *The Cost of Special Education* (Santa Monica, Calif.: The RAND Corporation, 1981); Richard A. Rossmiller, "Program Patterns and Expenditures for Special Education in Smaller School Districts," *Journal of Education Finance* 7 (Spring 1982), pp. 381–402.
11. Aaron S. Gurwitz, *The Economics of Public School Finance* (Cambridge: Ballinger Publishing Company, 1982), pp. 159–170; Jay C. Chambers, "The Development of a Cost of Education Index," *Journal of Education Finance* 5 (Winter 1980), p. 262–281.
12. John Augenblick, "Issues in School Finance" (Denver, Colo.: Augenblick, Van de Water & Associates, 1984), pp. 13–14.
13. Joan Scheuer, "The Equity of New York State's System of Financing Schools: An Update," *Journal of Education Finance* 9 (Summer 1983), pp. 83–84. See also G. Alan Hickrod, R.B. Chandhari, and B.C. Hubbad, "The Decline and Fall of School Finance Reform in Illinois," *Journal of Education Finance* 9 (Summer 1983), pp. 17–38.

STEVEN D. GOLD

State Aid for Local Schools:
Trends and Prospects

One of the most significant developments in state finances since 1970 has been the increase in state responsibility for financing local schools. The increase in the state share of school costs has been widely applauded for several reasons. It often increases school resources considerably, it tends to relieve pressure on property taxes, and it may reduce disparities among school districts. Recently, several states have carried this trend forward with general sales tax increases from which the revenue was earmarked for increased school aid. However, the prospect is not necessarily for a continuation of the increase in the state share of school costs. The growth of state aid slowed significantly in many states during the fiscal difficulties of the early 1980s; the size of future increases in state aid will be related to state fiscal conditions.

This article consists of two parts. First, the increase in the state share of school costs since 1970 is analyzed. Second, the major factors affecting future aid trends are discussed.

TRENDS IN STATE AID SINCE 1970

Table 1 shows the state, local, and federal shares of school revenue for various years since 1970. Clearly, the major trend has been for state aid to increase in relation to other revenue sources; however, this increase has been irregular. From 1980 to 1983, a period of serious state fiscal problems, the state share of nonfederal school revenue decreased slightly. (This development is obscured if federal aid is included because federal aid was decreasing in absolute terms.) The 1984 level of state support was lower than in 1980, but still considerably higher than in 1970. The long-term trend has been up, although the medium trend has been mildly down.

State-by-State Trends

In a sense it is misleading to speak of the national averages because there is so much diversity among states. The remainder of this section explores the dimensions of that

Steven D. Gold is senior fellow for fiscal affairs, National Conference of State Legislatures, Denver, Colorado.

TABLE 1
Federal, State, and Local Government Shares of
School Revenue, Selected Years, 1970–84
(percent)

Year	PERCENTAGE OF TOTAL REVENUE			PERCENTAGE OF NONFEDERAL REVENUE	
	Federal	State	Local	State	Local
1973–74	8.3	42.7	49.0	46.6	53.4
1974–75	8.1	43.6	48.4	47.4	52.6
1975–76	8.5	43.7	47.8	47.8	52.2
1976–77	8.4	43.8	47.8	47.8	52.2
1977–78	8.8	44.3	46.9	48.5	51.5
1978–79	8.8	47.3	43.9	51.9	48.1
1979–80	9.2	49.1	41.7	54.1	45.9
1980–81	8.7	48.5	42.8	53.2	46.8
1981–82	7.4	48.6	44.0	52.5	47.5
1982–83	6.8	48.4	44.8	51.9	48.1
1983–84	6.5	49.0	44.5	52.4	47.6

Note: Local revenue includes other revenue, such as local income from leases on school lands and miscellaneous sources (interest on bank deposits, tuition, gifts, school lunch charges, etc.) This table does not include nonrevenue receipts (loans, sales of bonds, sales of property purchased from capital funds, and insurance adjustments).

Source: National Education Association, *Estimates of School Statistics, 1983-84* (Washington, D.C.: NEA, April 1984).

---

diversity. Table 2 summarizes the differences among states in the state share of non-federal school revenue in 1984. At one extreme are Hawaii, New Mexico, and Alaska, where the state share exceeds 80 percent. At the other end of the continuum is New Hampshire, with a local share of more than 90 percent. Alaska and New Hampshire are the only states with neither a personal income nor a general sales tax. Alaska has enormous revenue because of its oil wealth, but New Hampshire's revenue is so meager that it cannot afford to provide much state aid to schools.

There are some clear regional patterns. The Southeast, Southwest, and Far West tend to have large state roles in financing schools, while the New England, Middle Atlantic, Great Lakes, and Plains states go in the other direction.

The year 1970 is a convenient starting point for examining recent trends because the years following it saw important changes in the school finance systems of many states. The prime motivators for these changes were: (1) the goal of relieving property taxes and (2) legal challenges (or the threat of such challenges) based on fiscal inequalities among school districts. At least 28 states have enacted major school finance reforms in the years since 1970.[1]

As Table 3 shows, many states significantly increased the state share of school costs between 1970 and 1984, although this trend was by no means universal. Twenty states increased their share of school costs at least 10 percentage points, while another 11 states had increases between 2 and 10 percentage points. But there were 12 states where

TABLE 2
State Share of Nonfederal School Revenue, 1983–84

Region	80 percent or more	70–80 percent	60–70 percent	50–60 percent	40–50 percent	40 percent or less
New England			Maine	Connecticut Massachusetts	Rhode Island Vermont	New Hampshire
Middle Atlantic		Delaware			Maryland New Jersey New York Pennsylvania	
Great Lakes				Indiana	Illinois Ohio	Michigan Wisconsin
Plains			North Dakota	Minnesota	Iowa Kansas Missouri	Nebraska South Dakota
Southeast		Alabama Kentucky	Arkansas Georgia Louisiana Mississippi North Carolina South Carolina West Virginia	Florida Tennessee	Virginia	
Southwest	New Mexico	Oklahoma		Arizona Texas		
Mountain			Idaho	Utah	Colorado Montana	Wyoming
Far West	Alaska Hawaii	California Washington			Nevada	Oregon

the state share was virtually unchanged (a difference of 2 percentage points), and in seven states the state share fell more than 2 percentage points.

There are several different explanations for why some states have had a decrease in the state share. Michigan had particularly acute fiscal problems; in addition, it provided substantial property tax relief through a large circuitbreaker (an approach that limits the burden of property taxes to a fixed portion of a family's income). North Carolina and Delaware began the period with relatively high state shares and were still well above average despite the slippage that occurred. Some other states followed tight-fisted spending policies in general and avoided the tax increases that would have allowed the state share to increase.

The picture looks different if one focuses on the four most recent years, from 1980 to 1984. This was a period of increasing fiscal stress. Although the economic recovery improved state finances in 1983, when states made their budget decisions for fiscal year 1984 the strength of the recovery was not yet apparent. The recession officially ended in December 1982; most state budgets were enacted by April 1983, and fiscal year 1984 began in July 1983 except in four states with different fiscal years.[2]

Only two states—Arizona and North Dakota—had increases in the state share of 10 percentage points or more during the early 1980s. As Table 4 shows, another 12 states had increases of more than 2 percentage points. Twenty-one states had increases or decreases of 2 percentage points or less, and 15 states had decreases of 2 percentage points or more. In other words, state fiscal austerity resulted in a decrease or no significant change in the state share in more than two-thirds of the 50 states.

Statistical Issues

Data on state aid is available from three sources—the National Education Association (NEA), the National Center for Education Statistics (NCES), and the U.S. Census Bureau.[3] The data from NEA and NCES are conceptually similar, but the NEA reports are more widely used because they are produced on a much more timely basis than those of NCES. Unfortunately, NEA's statistics are subject to some significant revisions in the year or two after they first appear. Several times recently revisions resulted in major changes in conclusions about what was happening in the school finance area. While this article uses NEA's data for the 1984 school year, past experience warns that it should be viewed with caution.

The Census Bureau's data differ in one very important respect from those of NEA and NCES. The latter two organizations consider only aid which passes directly from the state to school districts with the label "school aid," or something similar. This procedure ignores a substantial amount of aid provided indirectly through property tax credits. For example, if the state government pays 54 percent of each homeowner's property tax bill (up to $650) as in Minnesota, or 10 percent of all property tax bills, as in Ohio, it is indirectly relieving property tax payers of a portion of their school property taxes. This is particularly important because schools usually account for about half of

---

TABLE 3
Change in State Share of Nonfederal School Revenue,
1970–1984

Increased at least 10 percent (20 states): Alaska (10.0), California (32.6), Colorado (13.9), Connecticut (14.5), Idaho (27.7), Indiana (14.5), Iowa (14.2), Kentucky (14.3), Maine (18.4), Massachusetts (22.0), Montana (22.1), Nebraska (11.6), New Jersey (12.3), New Mexico (11.9), North Dakota (32.4), Ohio (16.5), Oklahoma (22.3), South Dakota (14.8), Washington (19.0), West Virginia (12.4)

Increased between 2 and 10 percent (11 states): Arizona (6.6), Arkansas (6.7), Hawaii (3.2), Illinois (4.0), Maryland (4.3), Minnesota (8.0), Missouri (6.4), Nevada (4.7), Oregon (8.4), Virginia (5.1), Wisconsin (7.2)

Increased or decreased by 2 percent or less (12 states): Alabama (0.9), Louisiana (1.1), Mississippi (2.0), Rhode Island (0.1), Utah (0.5), Kansas (0.0), Texas (0.0), Georgia (-0.6), New Hampshire (-1.3), Pennsylvania (-1.8), South Carolina (-1.9), Wyoming (-0.7)

Decreased by more than 2 percent (7 states): Delaware (-2.5), Florida (-2.2), Michigan (-10.2), New York (-5.8), North Carolina (-8.1), Tennessee (-3.5), Vermont (-2.4)

Source: Advisory Commission on Intergovernmental Relations, *Significant Features of Fiscal Federalism, 1982-83* (for 1970); National Education Association, *Estimates of School Statistics, 1983-84* (for 1984).

TABLE 4
Change in State Share of Nonfederal School Revenue,
1980–1984

Increased at least 10 percent (2 states): Arizona (10.3), North Dakota (12.6)

Increased between 2 and 10 percent (12 states): Alaska (4.6), Connecticut (6.2), Idaho (8.3), Louisiana (3.6), Massachusetts (4.4), Missouri (2.3), Nebraska (12.3), New Mexico (10.8), Oklahoma (6.9), South Dakota (5.1), Vermont (3.1), Washington (2.2)

Increased or decreased by 2 percent or less (21 states): Alabama (2.0), Arkansas (0.3), Colorado (0.5), Delaware (0.1), Hawaii (0.4), Maine (1.1), Maryland (0.3), New Jersey (0.4), South Carolina (0.7), Utah (0.8), West Virginia (0.2), Kansas (0.0), Indiana (-1.4), Iowa (-2.0), Kentucky (-0.4), Mississippi (-1.2), New Hampshire (-1.2), New York (-1.1), Pennsylvania (-1.7), Wisconsin (-0.2)

Decreased by more than 2 percent (15 states): California (-5.6), Florida (-4.3), Georgia (-2.9), Illinois (-2.7), Michigan (-13.9), Minnesota (-4.6), Montana (-4.1), Nevada (-19.3), North Carolina (-4.0), Ohio (-2.4), Oregon (-8.9), Rhode Island (-3.6), Tennessee (-5.2), Texas (-5.0), Wyoming (-5.7)

Source: Advisory Commission on Intergovernmental Relations, *Significant Features of Fiscal Federalism, 1982-83* (for 1970); National Educational Association, *Estimates of School Statistics, 1983-84* (for 1984).

---

the total property tax levy. NEA and NCES data make it appear as if those states which have chosen to provide a portion of their school aid through the property tax credit mechanism are offering less state aid than they actually are.

This distortion is particularly important in the states of Minnesota, Wisconsin, Michigan, and Oregon, because they have the largest property tax credit programs. It is also important in Ohio, Vermont, Indiana (in some years), Iowa, and New Jersey.

Another statistical problem which should be noted is common to all surveys about state finances. The state officials responding to the survey may be less careful in some states than others, resulting in occasional erroneous information. For example, the data from NCES and NEA for 1970 differ by several percentage points in many states. This article utilizes NEA data throughout.[4]

A final issue is whether to include federal aid in examining the state share of school costs. While it is appropriate to include federal aid in addressing certain issues, if the focus of a study is state-local relations, it is probably best to concentrate on the state share of *nonfederal* school revenue.

THE OUTLOOK FOR FUTURE STATE AID

State government aid for elementary and secondary education depends on the health of state finances and the priority accorded to school aid and property tax relief as opposed to other state fiscal objectives. The health of state finances depends on three considerations—the national economy, federal policy, and taxpayer willingness to pay taxes. Each of these factors will be considered in turn.

Before launching this discussion, one should emphasize the great uncertainty surrounding many of these issues. The period since 1978 has been a tumultuous one, with a battery of unusual forces buffeting state finances. First, the "tax revolt" led the majority of states to lower their taxes. Then the most severe recession in the last four decades placed state finances under extreme stress. On top of these developments, President Reagan reversed decades of federal policy by reducing aid to state and local governments. However, many of the president's far-reaching proposals for reform of the federal system were rejected by Congress or enacted in watered-down form. The major imponderables now are how high the economic growth rate will be, whether radical changes in federal aid policy will be enacted in 1985 or later years, and whether taxpayers will countenance significant further tax increases. On balance, one may predict that the 1986–88 period will be a troubled one for the finances of many states, which implies that aid to schools will continue under pressure. Aid will continue to increase, but it is unlikely to grow much faster than locally raised revenue in most states. The best that can be hoped for in most states is a gradual, moderate further increase in the state share.

The National Economy

National economic trends are crucially important for the fiscal health of state governments because they dictate the extent to which revenue will grow without increases in tax rates. Each state tax system has a certain income-elasticity, which expresses the percentage increase in revenue resulting from a one percent increase in personal income. For example, if the elasticity is 1.2, a 10 percent increase in income will raise revenue 12 percent. Because it is less politically painful for a state to obtain additional revenue automatically from economic growth (or inflation) than from a discretionary tax increase, economic conditions are an important determinant of state fiscal conditions.[5]

The performance of the national economy became progressively weaker from the late 1960s to the early 1980s. The rate of increase of productivity fell from 3.2 percent in 1948–65 to 2.3 percent in 1965–72, to 1.1 percent in 1972–78, and to even less in 1978–82.[6] This is important because the rate of productivity improvement is intimately associated with increases in real income. A large portion of the population had little improvement in their standard of living from 1973 to 1983 because of the sluggish growth of productivity and the redistribution of income resulting from higher energy prices and other factors.

The early 1980s were an especially dismal period for the economy. A sharp, brief recession in 1980 was followed by the shortest recovery in history and then, in 1981 and 1982, an extended recession sent unemployment rates to their highest levels since World War II.[7]

This extended recessionary period hit state finances particularly hard because the states were unprepared for it. In response to the tax revolt, many states had reduced the balances which they normally held as a precaution against economic adversity. Economic forecasters had failed to predict the onset of the 1981 recession; then they were wrong in predicting that it would end by the middle of 1982. The declining fortunes of the states are illustrated by their diminishing year-end balances. From $11.8 billion (9.4 percent of general fund spending) in 1980, they fell to $6.5 billion in 1981, $4.2

billion in 1982, and $2 billion (1.3 percent of spending) in 1983.[8] The economic recovery and tax increases have improved state fiscal conditions since early 1983, but balances are still far below their 1980 level.[9]

While the economic recovery has been more vigorous than most economists expected, it is premature to conclude that the long economic malaise which afflicted the nation from 1973 to 1982 is over. The federal deficit represents an enormous unresolved problem. The economy has so much momentum that a recession is unlikely before 1986, but many, if not most, economists foresee serious economic problems if the deficit is not brought under control. The extremely high level of real interest rates is likely to retard investment and distort the economy, and real interest rates are unlikely to decrease until the deficit is significantly reduced.[10]

Fiscal conditions in some states will be helped by their relatively strong economies. Massachusetts and New Jersey are examples of states where the growth outlook is much better than average. But the experience of the early 1980s suggests that when the economy is in a serious recession, few states avoid fiscal problems. In 1981 and 1982 the oil-producing states were an isolated island of strength, but because of decreasing oil prices they have been in the fiscal doldrums in 1983 and 1984.

Thus, the troubled economic outlook appears to have negative implications for state fiscal conditions.

The Federal Budget

Federal aid to state and local governments financed over one quarter of their total spending in 1978; that proportion was reduced to 20 percent in 1983. President Reagan's proposals would have dropped aid to about 3 or 4 percent of expenditures by 1991.[11] A decrease of that magnitude is extremely unlikely, but the outlook is that federal aid will continue to decline in importance as a revenue source for the states.

In nominal dollars, federal aid is expected to exceed its previous peak in fiscal year 1984, when it is projected to be $98.8 billion, compared to a previous high of $94.8 billion in 1981. But in real dollars, federal aid fell 13 percent between 1981 and 1984. Moreover, an ever-increasing proportion of federal aid is for grants to individuals, particularly Aid to Families with Dependent Children (AFDC) and Medicaid. Aid for government programs (rather than grants to individuals) diminished from 57.9 percent of the total in 1981 to 53.5 percent in 1984.[12]

Federal aid for education was the target of more than the average amount of reductions, with education spending falling from $7.0 billion in 1981 to $6.3 billion in 1983.[13] However, this direct loss of financial assistance is probably less significant for schools than the indirect impact of reduced federal aid on state budgets. Education will face increased competition for state dollars from social services, where the decrease in federal aid is likely to have a larger effect on state finances.

The paramount point is that the deficit problem looms so large that a significant increase in federal aid to education is out of the question. Rather, real aid decreases seem highly probable.

Taxpayer Attitude Toward State Tax Increases[14]

The status of the tax revolt defies simple characterization. Some articles in national media have declared its demise, but that may be premature. The tax revolt can be compared to a conflagration which swept across the country in the late 1970s and then gradually subsided. Its embers are still alive in some states and, under certain conditions, they could help to ignite widespread new fires.

After Proposition 13 was approved by California voters in June 1978, states went on a tax-cutting binge, with more than half of them reducing their sales or personal income taxes. For several years there were very few significant tax increases, but the inhibition against raising taxes gradually weakened. Although raising taxes was a last resort, most states eventually exhausted their other options and increased taxes significantly in 1982 or 1983. In fact, three-quarters of the states raised some taxes in 1983, with revenue boosted at least $7.5 billion on an annual basis.[15]

In 1984 no single consistent tax trend is apparent in the country. On the one hand, many of the states that raised taxes in 1982 or 1983 have at least partially rolled back those increases or allowed temporary increases to expire. On the other hand, a number of states which previously avoided tax increases, such as Oklahoma, Texas, South Carolina, and Tennessee, have increased taxes.

The experience of the past several years suggests that state policymakers believe that a majority of voters will support a tax increase if a strong case has been made that it is needed to avoid serious service reductions. But legislators and governors are wary of allowing large surpluses to accumulate and give the appearance that taxes have been raised excessively.

Tax protestors continue to place tax-cutting initiatives on state ballots. For example, this year voters are expected to decide on tax cuts proposed in Michigan, Oregon, California, and perhaps several other states. Based on the recent record, most of these initiatives are likely to be defeated because voters have strongly tended to reject radical tax-cutting initiatives (while approving more moderate proposals that limit the growth of taxes). However, if some of these measures are approved, they will generate a new wave of tax revolt enthusiasm which is likely to inhibit near-term tax increases throughout the country. There is a significant possibility that some of this year's tax revolt initiatives will be approved because they are less radical than measures rejected in the past and because some states have relatively large surpluses which could induce voters to be skeptical about predictions of service cutbacks if taxes are reduced.

Another factor that could discourage states from raising their taxes is possible federal tax increases. The federal government created a large amount of room for states to increase their taxes with its 25 percent income tax rate reduction in 1981–83, but now the odds favor significant federal tax increases to reduce the deficit. Much depends on the form which federal tax increases assume. If the federal government broadens its income tax base by eliminating deductions and exclusions from income, this would tend to boost state tax revenue since most states conform to such federal tax actions. On the other hand, if the federal government were to adopt a new consumption tax or increase income tax rates, this might tend to "crowd out" state efforts to increase their own taxes.

Attitudes toward tax increases are probably related to a factor discussed earlier, the performance of the national economy. If the economy performs well enough that average real incomes are rising, taxpayers should be more tolerant of tax increases. Under such a scenario, after-tax incomes could increase even though effective tax rates were rising. However, if economic growth is sluggish and real incomes are not on the upswing, resistance to tax increases is likely to stiffen.

Priority of School Aid

The three factors discussed above will determine the states' financial strength over the rest of the 1980s. From the viewpoint of school finance, a final crucial element is the priority accorded to helping elementary and secondary education.

Education is normally one of the strongest forces in the formulation of state budgets. In part, this is because polls usually show greater support for increased school spending than for any other state program. Another factor is that teachers' organizations frequently are among the most powerful interest groups in the state capitol. Evidence that this political clout has paid off is the fact that between 1970 and 1981, a period when public school enrollment dropped 10 percent, aid for education increased its share of general state spending.[16] This traditional political strength of school forces has been bolstered since education emerged suddenly as a "sexy issue" in 1983, with support from President Reagan and numerous national and state reports.

In recent years, whenever a state had a significant tax increase that was not justified by general budget problems, boosting support for education was the most important rationale. At least six states have raised their sales or income taxes since 1982 with school aid the primary beneficiary—Vermont, Missouri, Mississippi, Arkansas, South Carolina, and Tennessee. In addition, education was a major beneficiary of Texas's 1984 tax increase package and Florida's 1983 adoption of the unitary approach to corporation income taxation.

If schools are going to benefit from higher taxes to boost state aid, 1985 is a key year. The enhanced interest in schools came too late in 1983 to have much of a budgetary impact that year, and tax increases are normally avoided in election years like 1984.

If the relatively gloomy scenario sketched in the previous sections of this article is accurate, the competition for state funds will be keen. This makes education's relative priority especially important.

Attitude Toward the Property Tax

One of the major reasons why states have assumed a greater proportion of school costs is a desire to decrease reliance on the property tax, which has long been regarded as one of the least popular of all taxes. Despite the enormous inflation in the values of homes and other kinds of property during the 1970s, most states shifted their tax systems significantly away from the property tax during that decade. For example, between 1972 and 1982, property tax revenue fell from $46.77 to $34.05 per $1,000 of personal income, while the average effective property tax rate on homes decreased from 2.12 percent to 1.26 percent.[17]

Resistance to the property tax weakened, however, in the early 1980s. In both 1981 and 1982 property tax collections rose at more than a 10 percent annual rate. The reasons for the resurgence of the property tax are not clear, although it probably had something to do with restrictions on state aid to local governments and the lagged effects of the inflation of the 1970s on assessed valuation. In any event, the rate of property tax increases has receded, and in 1983 it fell to 7.3 percent.[18]

Most observers of state finances regard it as very unlikely that property taxes will be allowed to grow at a high rate for a sustained period of time. If this is accurate, it implies that the state share of school costs will not fall much, unless local nonproperty taxes come into wider use, which is also unlikely. An expansion and tightening of state-imposed limits on school spending and taxes could occur if state officials reject both higher property taxes and boosts in state aid.

CONCLUSION

States have been assuming a greater role in financing schools, although there was some backsliding in the early 1980s. The outlook for further substantial increases over the next five years is not bright. Unless the economy performs much better than it has since oil prices shot up in 1973, many states are likely to experience a degree of fiscal stress, exacerbated by tight-fisted federal aid policies. In such an environment, large increases in the state share of school costs are unlikely.

With state finances still relatively healthy and enthusiasm for education reform still strong, 1985 may be the year that offers the best chance for big increases in school aid for some time.

NOTES

The views expressed are solely those of the author and do not necessarily reflect the position of NCSL.
1. Allan Odden and John Augenblick, *School Finance Reform in the States: 1981* (Denver: Education Commission of the States, 1981).
2. New York (April 1), Texas (September 1), Alabama (October 1), and Michigan (October 1).
3. National Education Association, *Estimates of School Statistics*; National Center for Education Statistics, *The Condition of Education*; and U.S. Census Bureau, *Governmental Finances*.
4. The U.S. Advisory Commission on Intergovernmental Relations (ACIR) report, *Significant Features of Fiscal Federalism, 1982–83 Edition*, p. 28, provides NEA data through 1983, but it has erroneous data for several states in 1970. Susan Carmon-Gerwirtz of NEA supplied the author with the latest revised NEA data.
5. Wallace E. Oates, "Automatic Increases in Tax Revenues—The Effect on the Size of the Public Budget," in W.E. Oates, ed., *Financing the New Federalism* (Baltimore: John Hopkins Press, 1975).
6. Lester C. Thurow, *Zero-Sum Society* (New York: Basic Books, 1980), p. 85; Council of Economic Advisers, *Economic Report of the President* (February 1984), p. 266.

7. Steven D. Gold, "State Fiscal Policy During the Recent Recession," in J. Palmer and I. Sawhill, eds., *Reagan and the States* (Washington, D.C.: The Urban Institute, 1984).

8. National Governors' Association and National Association of State Budget Officers, *Fiscal Survey of the States: 1984* (Washington, D.C., 1984), p. 2.

9. Steven Gold and Corina Eckl, *State Budget Actions in 1984* (Denver: National Conference of State Legislatures, 1984).

10. Alice Rivlin, ed., *Economic Choices: 1984* (Washington, D.C.: Brookings Institution, 1984).

11. U.S. Commerce Department, *Survey of Current Business* (May 1984), p. 7; George Peterson, "The State and Local Sector," in John L. Palmer and Isabel V. Sawhill, eds., *The Reagan Experiment* (Washington, D.C.: The Urban Institute, 1982), p. 159.

12. U.S. Office of Management and Budget, "Special Analysis H," *Budget of the United States Government, FY 1985: Special Analyses*, p. H-17. The price index used is the implicit deflator for state and local governments.

13. The figures on education spending are the federal outlays for elementary, secondary, and vocational education, so they may include some spending not specifically for aid. The expenditures are the actual 1981 and 1983 outlays as reported in the federal budgets for FY 1983 and FY 1985.

14. This section draws heavily on Steven Gold, "State Tax Increases of 1983: Prelude to Another Tax Revolt?" *National Tax Journal* xxvii (March 1984), pp. 9–22.

15. Steven D. Gold and Karen M. Benker, *State Budget Actions in 1982* (Denver: National Conference of State Legislatures, 1983).

16. Steven D. Gold, "Recent Developments in State Finances," *National Tax Journal* xxxvi (March 1983), p. 17.

17. Steven Gold, "Patterns of Financing Local Services" (Denver: National Conference of State Legislatures, 1984).

18. Steven Gold, "State Tax Revenues Rebound," Tax Notes (July 16, 1984), pp. 307–308.

RICHARD H. GOODMAN

Providing Adequate Resources for Public Elementary and Secondary Schools

During the last twenty years, policymakers have been preoccupied with education equity issues, including the expansion of access, the provision of equal opportunity, and the fairness of resource allocation. Recently, the attention of policymakers has turned to the adequacy of education support. What is an "adequate" education in our nation's public elementary/secondary schools? Does America have enough resources to provide such an education to all its children? This article will discuss five areas related to these questions, concluding with ideas on what can be done to assure the availability of adequate resources for education in the future. The five areas are:

1. What are public schools expected to do?
2. What resources do they have to get the job done?
3. What does it cost? How do costs differ among states, and among school districts within a state?
4. Does money make a difference in the adequacy of education?
5. Can America afford to provide an adequate education for all its children?

WHAT ARE PUBLIC ELEMENTARY AND SECONDARY SCHOOLS EXPECTED TO DO?

America's public schools today are expected to do more for all children than ever before in our history. The traditional task included teaching the "3 R's," history, geography, science, character development, and self-reliance. As recently as 1950, only about 50 percent of our youth graduated from high school; others dropped out at age 16 to go to work. While the total public school enrollment has declined in recent years, from a high of over 46 million children in 1971 to around 40 million in 1981, the percentage of children ages 5–17 in school has increased from 83 percent in 1950 to nearly 90 percent today.[1]

The public schools are expected to prepare youth for college, work, the military, and homemaking. High school graduates are expected to be competent in reading, writing, and computing, as well as to be good citizens, to know how to drive, and to be familiar

Richard H. Goodman is director, Center for Educational Field Services, and executive director, New Hampshire Association of School Boards.

with modern health concepts. While the expectations for high school graduates has grown, there has been an upheaval in the American family. In 1970 about eight million children were living with only one parent. By 1980 the number had grown to 13 million children. The National Education Association projects that nearly half the children born in 1980 will live in single-parent families before they turn 18. There has been a sharp rise in the dropout rate from 1972 to 1982; only 72.8 percent of high school students graduated in 1982 compared to 77.2 percent in 1972. The result is a demand for more school programs in areas such as drug and alcohol education, sex and health education, and guidance.

Are public schools expected to do more than is reasonable? What is the role of education in a pluralistic, technological society? Since World War II, America has placed many new demands on its public schools. For example, the typical high school today includes laboratories for biology, chemistry, and physics; some schools even offer college-level science. Today's students are learning to use word processors and computers. They may choose to study one or more foreign languages. Advanced mathematics students will learn calculus before they go to college. Increasingly, schools provide a variety of courses in English and the social studies, with greater focus on writing. Students may begin to learn a trade in vocational centers that should have the same equipment used by business firms. Some students leave school for several hours each day to participate in a supervised on-the-job work experience.

Over the past decade, following the passage of Public Law 94–142 by the U.S. Congress, programs for the handicapped have increased dramatically. Elevators and ramps have been installed in schools. Children once isolated either in special schools or in a separate room are now mainstreamed into regular classes. Operating under the philosophy that all children can learn, today's schools include large numbers of special education teachers and other experts trained to work with handicapped children.

The variety of extracurricular activities has also increased in recent years. In addition to sports teams, music ensembles, a school paper, and a student government, schools offer activities ranging from computer to chess to photography clubs. In order to promote equal opportunities, schools provide athletic facilities and experiences for girls that match those for boys.

Perhaps because of the new demands on education, there is increasing conflict over what the public schools should do. College and university education has become so commonplace that schools focus a great deal of their resources on precollege training. In high schools it is rare to find many students who will not complete at least three years of mathematics; three or four years of a foreign language; three years of science that include biology, chemistry, or physics (plus another course such as astronomy, earth science, or geology); two or three years of social studies, including a year-long course in U.S. history; and four years of English. Many students also take at least one year of art and music. A recent study illustrates that many states have significantly increased graduation requirements to insure that all students have a common core of essential courses.[3]

Pre-vocational training is now as commonplace as precollege training in many high

TABLE 1
Percentage Distribution of School Expenditures,
1949–50 and 1979–80

Purpose of Expenditure	1949–50	1979–80
Administration	3.8	4.4
Instruction	53.3	55.5
Plant operational maintenance	11.0	10.2
Fixed charges	4.5	12.3
Other school services	7.7	8.3
Capital outlay	17.4	6.8
Interest on school debt	1.7	2.0
All other	0.6	0.5
Total	100.0	100.0

Source: Digest of Education Statistics, U.S. Department of Education, National Center for Education Statistics, 1982.

---

schools. Because of the demand for secretaries, almost every high school has a business education program with courses in typing, stenography, bookkeeping, and, in recent years, word processing. Larger high schools and vocational schools offer a much richer array of courses.

While states are increasing the job of the schools by imposing new mandates, several national spokespersons argue for specifying goals that are clearly tied to the fundamental mission of educating youth. One of America's distinguished scholars, Dr. Theodore Sizer, argues that "education of the intellect is one obvious mandate of the public school system."[4] He further argues that schools have another "inescapable" purpose—an education in character. Finally, he states that literacy, numeracy, and civic understanding are all essential primary goals of a public school education.

Dr. Ernest Boyer, a former U.S. commissioner of education and now president of the Carnegie Foundation for the Advancement of Teaching, recommends that two-thirds of the high school program be required to promote a core of common learning that includes math, science, language and literature, the arts, human heritage, and non-Western culture. He advocates requiring students to perform a term of voluntary service before they graduate, such as working in a hospital, a nursing home, or another community-based organization.

Most Americans agree with Harvard University's former president, James Bryant Conant, who argued for a comprehensive high school. Since public schools are to be what the voters in our democracy want them to be, the schools are expected to provide a wide array of programs so the American dream of equal opportunity for all can be achieved.

WHAT RESOURCES DO THE SCHOOLS HAVE TO GET THE JOB DONE?

Although demands on schools have changed, the technology of providing services has not. Staff, textbooks, equipment, and facilities are still the resources required to edu-

TABLE 2
Estimated Average Salaries of Instructional
Staff in Public Schools, 1982–83

1. Alaska	$34,510	25. Indiana	20,873
2. California	27,553	26. Ohio	20,730
3. District of Columbia	26,922	27. Montana	20,150
4. Nevada	26,412	28. Texas	20,092
5. New York	25,600	29. Louisiana	19,749
6. Hawaii	25,423	30. Florida	19,605
7. Washington	24,470	31. Iowa	19,538
8. Wyoming	23,820	32. Virginia	19,492
9. Maryland	23,773	33. Kentucky	19,230
10. Michigan	23,744	34. Kansas	19,169
11. Rhode Island	23,600	35. South Carolina	18,980
12. Illinois	23,347	36. Oklahoma	18,870
13. Minnesota	23,313	37. North Dakota	18,830
14. Massachusetts	23,000	38. Nebraska	18,488
15. Utah	22,768	39. Alabama	18,450
16. New Jersey	22,684	40. North Carolina	18,327
17. Wisconsin	22,356	41. Georgia	18,282
18. Colorado	22,291	42. Idaho	18,229
19. Arizona	22,000	43. Missouri	18,216
20. Pennsylvania	21,800	44. West Virginia	18,054
21. Connecticut	21,770	45. Tennessee	17,743
		46. South Dakota	16,493
U.S. average	21,671	47. Maine	16,205
		48. New Hampshire	15,616
22. Oregon	21,460	49. Arkansas	15,549
23. Delaware	21,333	50. Vermont	15,003
24. New Mexico	21,168	51. Mississippi	14,824

Source: National Education Association, *Ranking of the States, 1983.*

---

cate our children—though there are signs that the computer may bring about new approaches to education.

But if the basic resources are essentially the same, the way in which schools deploy these resources is not. A century ago, staff meant classroom teachers and a principal. Today's schools require a relatively large number of specialists. Over the years, many schools across the nation recognized the need for specialists to work with handicapped children, including speech therapists and psychologists. A post World War II America demanded that the schools provide hot lunch programs, driver education, library-media centers, foreign language laboratories, and guidance counselors.

Looking at how the school dollar is spent gives one a bird's-eye view of the resources needed in education. The National Center for Education Statistics keeps track of school expenditures each year. Over $100 billion was spent for public elementary and secondary education in 1982–83. It is instructive to examine how the dollars are spent. Expenditure data for 1949–50 and 1979–80 are displayed in Table 1.

The data illustrate that staff and instructional materials are the major cost. Capital outlay (primarily new buildings) has taken a diminishing share annually as the post-World War II "baby boom" impact on schools ended. Other than the capital outlay decreases, the only significant change is in fixed charges, which includes insurance and fringe benefits. Most of the expenditure items are relatively unchanged in proportional allocation.

WHAT DOES EDUCATION COST? HOW DO COSTS DIFFER AMONG STATES, AND AMONG SCHOOL DISTRICTS WITHIN A STATE?

In 1982–83, an average of $2,952 per pupil was spent on public education; 23 states and the District of Columbia spent more, with Alaska the top spender at $6,301 per pupil, followed by New York at $4,303.[5] Alabama spent the lowest amount, $1,546 per pupil. After adjusting for inflation, this compares with an average of $1,312 per pupil 20 years earlier. Most of the money is spent on salaries for the instructional staff. The average annual teacher salary was $20,336 in 1979–80, a drop from $22,028 (in 1979–80 dollars) a decade earlier.[6] The average salary in 1982–83 was only $21,671. Table 2 shows the vast differences in salaries for instructional staff among the states.

While per-pupil costs (largely determined by instructional salaries) vary a great deal among the states, one also finds that costs vary a great deal within a state. In New Hampshire, a recent study by the State Department of Education shows variations in the per-pupil costs for elementary schools, middle and junior high schools, and high schools. The wide range is illustrated in Table 3.

What do these cost differences mean? What might explain the differences? Tastes? Pupil needs? Local ability to pay? State and federal support? The next section discusses whether money makes a difference in the adequacy of education.

DOES MONEY MAKE A DIFFERENCE IN THE ADEQUACY OF EDUCATION?

In public education the political process is relied upon to produce adequacy.[7] Through the actions of state legislatures, state education boards and agencies, and local school boards, the general public defines adequacy.

Adequacy in many states is established by legislative decree. Minimum standards for graduation may include four years of English, one year of U.S. history, and two years

---

TABLE 3
Expenditures Per Pupil for Current Operating Expenses,
New Hampshire Public Schools, 1982–83

	Elementary School	Middle–Junior High School	High School
Low	$979	$1,261	$1,432
Average	2,093	2,338	2,517
High	5,754	2,517	5,556

Source: New Hampshire State Department of Education.

TABLE 4
Per-Pupil Costs for Selected New Hampshire High Schools, 1982–83

School	High School Enrollment	1982–83 Per-Pupil Cost*
Concord	1,120	$3229
Rochester	1,129	$2071
Peterborough	721	$3031
Penacook	643	$1856
Whitefield	450	$3177
Raymond	420	$2428
Hopkinton	272	$2956
Farmington	321	$1702

*Per pupil cost includes all operating expenses except capital outlays, transportation, and debt obligations. Based on 1982–83 data submitted to State Department of Education.

Source: "Does Money Make a Difference in the Quality of High School Education?" Center for Educational Field Services (Durham, N.H.: University of New Hampshire, 1984), monograph.

each of mathematics and science. In the state of Washington, the legislature has specified the number of instructional hours per year in the required subjects. In other states, a required examination defines adequate education. Who would question whether or not the student who passes the New York Regents exam had an adequate education? The nation's colleges and universities consider each applicant's score on the Scholastic Aptitude Test (SAT) or the American College Testing Program (ACT) exam as a predictor of aptitude for college work. But minimum standards, legislative requirements, or test scores, alone or in combination, are imperfect descriptors of adequacy in public education.

An adequate education requires money—money for a competent staff of teachers. Money for a principal who understands youth and how to run an effective school. Money for the diversity of programs, books, and facilities required to enable some students to be trained for employment immediately after graduation, others for further education.

Is there sufficient money to enable all public schools in our nation to be adequate schools? This question assumes that some schools are inadequate. Let us examine the assumption before addressing the question.

During the past 18 months many prominent citizens, including leading businessmen and politicians, have examined the education system and, because of the inadequacies of our schools, have declared our country to be "a nation at risk."[8] Panels and commissions have eloquently reported that our economy is faltering,[9] that we have fallen behind other nations in educating youth in science and technology,[10] and that our high schools in particular need a massive overhaul.[11] Each report, in its own unique way, has sounded a clarion call to educators and politicians, businessmen and parents, voters and students, to take steps to restore quality to our schools if our democracy is to survive and flourish.

A blue-ribbon committee of 12 citizens in New Hampshire has recently completed a study to answer the question: "does money make a difference in the quality of high school education?"[12] The committee defined quality education as "the extent to which a school contributes to the academic, vocational, and personal development of students." The citizens were drawn from business and industry, higher education, parents, public and private schools, and state government. Through classroom observations, interviews with students, parents, teachers, and administrators, and examination of documents, they formed impressions of school quality. While the judgments reached are subjective, they are nonetheless significant because they represent the combined efforts of a diverse, conscientious, and capable group of citizens. Eight schools were studied in four "matched pairs." Each pair had to be of similar size, with one spending considerably more than the other. The sizes and per-pupil costs of the schools are presented in Table 4.

One central question guided the inquiry: does money make a difference? Are there identifiable differences in the quality of education in the schools that are the result of the level of financial support the school receives? The blue-ribbon committee summarized its 27-page report as follows:

Although there are several nonmonetary factors that also influence school quality, it is our belief, based on what we saw, that money makes a significant difference in determining the quality of high school education in schools of comparable size. A summary of our major findings concerning monetary factors follows:

1. Schools will face increasing difficulty attracting and holding the best teachers and principals. The teachers are subsidizing the schools. The problem is especially serious in the low-expenditure schools where many teachers must have a second job in order to continue teaching. This takes teacher time and energy from education at a time when the schools need their help more than ever.
2. Because other careers have become more desirable, the number of talented dedicated persons preparing to be teachers continually declines. This is especially true of women, who now have a very wide range of attractive career choices. Thus, competition for teachers will increase and the low expenditure school districts will be even less able to compete for the best.
3. Schools with low expenditures tend to be in communities where educational expectations are also low. Local traditions, values, and cultural patterns do little to reinforce and extend the academic goals of the school. Yet it is the schools in these communities that are least able to compensate for these limitations.
4. Schools with low expenditures are limited in virtually every dimension: a narrow range of subjects taught, inadequate instructional equipment, insufficient supplies, poor physical facilities, and unsatisfactory working conditions for students and teachers. These problems are especially serious in the smaller, low expenditure schools, although economies of scale make it possible for larger low expenditure schools to respond effectively to some of these limitations.
5. By the few measures available, educational attainments of students in low expenditure schools are below those of students in the high expenditure schools.

Clearly the most important factor in determining the adequacy of education is the quality of the teaching and administrative staff. The New Hampshire study found that

TABLE 5
Personal Consumption:
Expenditures For Selected Luxury Items, 1983
($ billions)

1. Drugs, sundries	$21.7
2. Liquor	50.9
3. Jewelry	12.9
4. Tobacco	28.3
5. Recreation (includes sports, movies, theater, TV, betting, etc.)	136.3
Total	230.1

Source: Bureau of Economic Analysis, U.S. Department of Commerce (National Income and Product Accounts).

---

in the more affluent schools three times as many teachers held advanced graduate degrees and almost twice as many had ten or more years of teaching experience. Teacher turnover was twice as high in the poorly supported schools. It is common to hear the complaint in low-spending, low-paying districts that "we are just a training ground for the better-paying schools."

In addition to the differences between the low-spending and high-spending schools with regard to the overall adequacy of the professional staff, the New Hampshire citizens also found that money makes a significant difference in the adequacy of the textbooks, school library, and equipment for science, industrial and fine arts, and business education. Overall working conditions are poorer in the low-spending schools, with many teachers required to teach a greater variety of courses with less supervisory assistance and little if any staff and curriculum development opportunities.

The New Hampshire study concluded by stating that:

> In summary, we point out, first, that school quality is a consequence of many influences. Money is definitely one of these. Community and family values; administrative leadership; faculty expectations, commitment and quality; the range of educational opportunities; and school size are also key factors that influence school quality. Second, we report that our visits and our study decisively support the conclusion that higher levels of financial expenditures for a school lead to more and better educational opportunities for students and these, in turn, lead to better educational quality. Thus we conclude that money wisely used makes a difference in the quality of high school education.

IS THERE SUFFICIENT MONEY FOR PUBLIC SCHOOLS TO PROVIDE AN ADEQUATE EDUCATION FOR ALL YOUTH IN AMERICA?

In 1983 Americans spent $126.8 billion for public elementary and secondary education.[13] In the same year, Americans spent $230.1 billion for luxury items as displayed in Table 5.

We are a wealthy nation. We have enough money to pay for what we need. The issue is whether or not we value education highly enough that we are willing to pay more in taxes for schools, which may mean that we will have less for cosmetics, liquor, smoking, sporting events, gambling, entertainment, etc.

Public education is a state responsibility. The state-local partnership in funding education varies a great deal across the nation. In New Hampshire, the reliance on local support is the highest in the nation at about 85 percent; the state provides about 8 percent of all funds, and the balance comes from the federal government. In Hawaii, at the other extreme, the state pays nearly 100 percent of the costs.[14]

Whether or not we can afford to provide an adequate education for all our youth depends in large measure on the tax capacity of each state. It also depends on the willingness of state legislators and governors to use their state's tax capacity for public education. In New Hampshire and other states which rely heavily on the local property tax, it depends on the willingness of local voters to levy higher taxes on their property, and on local desires regarding the scope and quality of public education. It also depends on the role the federal government is willing to play in financing education. For example, when P.L. 94–142 was passed in 1975, state and local educators were told the federal government would pay 40 percent of the annual cost of educating handicapped children; actually only about 9 percent of the cost is paid by the federal government.

Increasingly, mandates from both the federal and state governments have driven up the costs of education. In New Hampshire, the mandates of P.L. 94–142 and state requirements to provide education and related services to handicapped youth ages 3–21 has created tremendous pressures on local voters. For example, one New Hampshire school district appropriated $60,000 to replace some of its old, broken-down classroom equipment this year, but unbudgeted increases in costs for special education forced the school board to reassign those funds to pay the deficit in special education. One might argue that the voters should tax themselves more heavily to provide an adequate education to all their children. Another might argue that the state has a responsibility to pay a higher share of educational costs in a relatively small and poor community. Yet another could make the case for the state to require consolidation of such small, poor schools to provide a more cost-efficient program.

WHAT CAN BE DONE TO ASSURE ADEQUATE RESOURCES FOR PUBLIC EDUCATION IN THE FUTURE?

All levels of government, business and industry, higher education, and enlightened citizens have major roles to play to assure adequate resources for public schools. There is no single source of adequate resources for public education.

Local, state, and federal taxes will continue to be the main sources of revenue for schools. But significant changes in tax policies are essential if America is to provide an adequate education for all its children.

The property tax should be available for local use to whatever extent the local taxpayers desire. Tax caps for education such as Proposition 13 in California and 2½ in Massachusetts should be repealed. If citizens are willing to pay more for local education than state government advocates, they should have that right. Yet at the same time, state government must provide a foundation level to assure that every student will receive an adequate education no matter where the student lives. States are now using a wide variety of taxes to fund state government. Governors and legislators must agree that adequate funding of public education will become a top priority, and ensure that the state distributes funds to local districts which have a combination of the greatest pupil need, lowest relative tax capacity, and reasonable local tax effort.

Business and industry also have a key role in providing adequate resources for public education and a major stake in the quality of our schools. North Carolina's Governor James B. Hunt, Jr., chairman of the Task Force on Economic Growth has said:

> The fundamental belief of the members of our task force was that education is the key to economic growth in this nation. Our charge was to make the public aware of the link between good schools and good jobs. And our ultimate goal was the renewal of a commitment to excellence in education.
>
> We also recommend the creation of partnerships between education, business, and government to improve education for economic growth. A central element of our plan is the involvement of business as a genuine partner with the schools, to help determine what is taught, to assist in marshaling the resources needed to provide top-quality education, and to convey to educators the skills that are needed in the workplace. Because we are preparing young people for the jobs of tomorrow, we must make business a full partner in educating those young people. We must tell the business community that, if it wants better employees and higher profits, it must be involved in what the schools teach and how they teach it.[15]

Business and industry can help in many ways at the local school level. They can provide summer jobs for teachers of subjects directly applicable to the business or industry. An obvious example is computer-related work for math teachers. They can loan skilled employees to teach part time in the schools. They can provide equipment. Corporations have "adopted" schools in several large cities, opening a myriad of opportunities for students and teachers, including on-the-job training for some students.

The major resource for an adequate education is the instructional staff. Attracting and keeping high-quality classroom teachers will continue to be a major problem and must become a top priority. In a recent *Phi Delta Kappan* article, Ernest Boyer writes:

> Surveys reveal that teachers are deeply troubled not only about salaries but also about their loss of status, the bureaucratic pressures, their negative public image, and the lack of recognition and rewards. To talk about recruiting better students into teaching without first examining the current circumstances that discourage teachers is simply a diversion. In 1983 we discovered that the push for excellence in education must begin by confronting those conditions that drive good teachers from the classroom in the first place.
>
> . . .Teachers cannot be expected to exhibit a high degree of professional competence when they are accorded such a low degree of professional treatment in their workaday world. Nor can we expect to attract the best and the brightest students into teaching when they have had 12 years of opportunity to observe firsthand the daily frustrations and petty humiliations that many teachers must endure. . . .
>
> In 1982 the average starting salary for teachers with bachelor's degrees was $12,769. When average starting salaries for teachers are compared to starting salaries of other professionals with bachelor's degrees, the contrast is striking. For engineers, the starting salary is $22,368; for computer scientists, $20,364.[16]

Some states and a few school districts are taking steps to employ their best teachers year round, thereby raising their salaries and providing them more prestige and recognition. But the problem of attracting high-quality people to teaching remains a critical one.

To attract bright high school and college students into teaching, the federal government should establish a special scholarship program to be administered by colleges and universities throughout the nation. Limited to the top 50 percent of each class, the federal scholarships for teaching would cover the major costs of education including tuition, room and board, and textbooks for five years. Students would earn the bachelor's degree in their major field of interest and the master's degree in teaching. They would work in schools part time during their training and, after graduation, be required to teach one year for every year they were on full scholarship. If they did not stay in teaching at least five years, they would repay a portion of the funds they received.

State and local governments would have to cooperate to develop teacher pay plans whereby teaching would be more competitive with other professions. While people do not become teachers primarily for the money, they should not have to hold a second job in order to fed and clothe their families and live at a respectable middle-class level.

America has enough money to pay its quality teachers a decent salary. Whether we will or not depends on how much the people and our elected representatives at all levels of government value education. Public expenditures for education were 5.9 percent of the U.S. gross national product in 1980 compared to 7.2 percent in Russia, 7.7 percent in Canada, 8.8 percent in Norway, and 9.1 percent in Sweden.[17] While no one enjoys paying more taxes, it is clear from the earlier discussion that billions of dollars are spent annually for luxury items. A federal tax on such items could provide the money needed to fund a national teaching scholarship program. If those who smoke, drink, gamble, attend sporting events, etc., paid an additional tax of .5 percent, over a billion dollars would be generated. At an average cost of $10,000 per student, this could support about 20,000 scholarships (of five years each) to lure the best qualified individuals to teaching.

Enlightened citizens are the nation's greatest untapped resource for public education. America needs more citizens who truly want to improve the quality of public education who will give time, the most precious resource of all. People who care about quality education need to make a decision to serve where it counts—on local school boards and in state legislatures. Nearly all policies that affect the funding of education are made at the state level and implemented locally. If America can produce enough citizens who care about children and the future of our society, our public schools—and our nation—will prosper.

NOTES

1. *Digest of Education Statistics, 1983–84*, Table 21 (Washington, D.C.: National Center for Education Statistics).
2. *NEA Today*, April 1983.
3. *The Condition of Education, 1984 Edition*, Table S11.

4. Theodore R. Sizer, *Horace's Compromise—The Dilemma of The American High School* (Boston: Houghton Mifflin Co., 1984), p. 84.
5. *Ranking of the States, 1983* (Washington, D.C.: National Education Association), Table H-10, p. 56; C-19, p. 25.
6. *Digest of Education Statistics, 1983–84*, Table 47.
7. James W. Guthrie, "Funding an 'Adequate Education,'" in *Standard Education Almanac 1983–84* (Chicago: Marquis Professional Publications).
8. The National Commission on Excellence in Education, *A Nation at Risk: The Imperative for Educational Reform* (Washington, D.C.: U.S. Department of Education, 1983).
9. *Action for Excellence* (Denver: Education Commission of the States, 1983).
10. National Science Board, *Educating Americans for the 21st Century* (Washington, D.C.: National Science Foundation, 1983).
11. Ernest Boyer, *High School* (New York, N.Y.: Harper and Row, 1983).
12. "Does Money Make a Difference in the Quality of High School Education?" monograph by the Center for Educational Field Services (Durham, N.H.: University of New Hampshire, 1984).
13. National Education Association, *Estimates of School Statistics, 1983–84*.
14. *Ranking of the States, 1983*, Table F-6, p. 43.
15. *Phi Delta Kappan*, April 1984, pp. 538–541.
16. *Phi Delta Kappan*, April 1984, pp. 525–530.
17. UNESCO Statistical Yearbook, reported in *Digest of Educational Statistics, 1983–84*, Table 165.

MICHAEL J. MURPHY

The Impact of Collective Bargaining on School Management and Governance

Collective bargaining between teachers and school districts has become a routine feature of the educational landscape. Since 1962 over ten thousand school districts have adopted collective bargaining as the mechanism for deciding certain work rules. More than 80 percent of all teachers now work in districts where a labor agreement is bilaterally negotiated. Currently about three quarters of the country's 16,000 school districts bargain with teachers' unions; most that do not are small or located in the three states where collective bargaining is severely restricted or prohibited by law. During most of the last twenty years collective bargaining has been a major issue. Much thought and study has been given to identifying changes in American schools that might result from collective bargaining. There has been much speculation about the probable effects of collective bargaining on teachers, teaching, and school district management. Teachers' unions have been blamed for many of the ills of American education just as trade unions have been charged with being the major contributor to failure in American heavy industry.

For two decades it has been forecast that major disruptions in educational practices would result from strong teachers' unions and the practice of collective bargaining. Many have said that without strong public controls teachers' unions would drive educational costs to intolerable levels by holding children hostage. Others have argued that parents and citizens would be shut out of their rightful place of influence in educational policy making. Administrators have said that collective bargaining would erode legitimate administrative authority and render change impossible.

Most claims about collective bargaining are overstated. Many of the charges have been accepted as true without a careful examination of data. Furthermore, these accusations carry a side message of distrust in teachers and their organizations, an allegation of unfitness to participate in decisions and to pursue intelligent policies that work toward the welfare of schools and school children.

This paper is an attempt to examine the evidence that has been collected about teacher collective bargaining over the past 20 years, and to draw some conclusions about its impact on school management and school governance. It is also an attempt to

Michael J. Murphy is professor, School of Education, University of Utah.

set a context that allows us to see how collective bargaining fits with other organizational processes.

VIEWS OF COLLECTIVE BARGAINING

Most educational researchers and practitioners view collective bargaining in isolation, as though it were something entirely new and unrelated to other aspects of teaching and administration, something like an organizational wart which appeared suddenly, whose cause is unknown and whose treatment is in doubt.

The reality is that union organization and collective bargaining are always a reaction to conditions in the work place; they come about as employees try to manage their work environment.[1] In the past unionization and collective bargaining were the result of workers' attempts to cope with factory life. Today it is more likely to be a reaction to poor management or decisional deprivation. Because of a tremendous power imbalance between the individual worker and the manager, workers must resort to collective strength to have an impact.

Although teachers have never been treated to the extreme dislocation and disorientation that resulted from the spread of the factory system of mass production, there has been a steady trend toward larger schools and school systems. Coupled with the growth and separation of administration, teachers have found their work becoming increasingly controlled and bureaucraticized. Individual teachers, facing increasing levels of management and a growing sense of powerlessness, have resorted to collective action for impact.

Most recent surveys indicate that teachers are not satisfied with their jobs. Teachers are unwilling to recommend teaching as a career to their children or to their students, and a large number of teachers report that if they had to do it over they would not become teachers. By all indications, teachers are unhappy about the conditions under which they serve. In particular they are concerned about their wage levels, their teaching loads, lack of community and student respect, and the number of nonteaching or clerical duties that they must assume. Teachers have turned to unions to remedy some of these concerns.

In a more positive view, collective bargaining may be seen as a process of employees gaining a "voice" in important decisions in the work place. A number of observers of work organizations have noted that over time there has been movement toward democratization, mirroring the trend in political government. Others have talked about the concept of "industrial democracy," which refers to mechanisms that employees use to participate in work and policy decisions.[2]

In the United States the right of employees to participate in decisions which affect their work existence is guaranteed by law. The National Labor Relations Act, known as the Wagner Act of 1935, guarantees workers in the private sector the right to organize into unions unfettered by management interference. Once organized and certified, employers must meet with the union to negotiate wages, hours, and conditions of employment. These issues are mandatory bargaining items. Though the Wagner Act is not designed to give workers a dominant voice in determining conditions of service or to assure that they will always receive the treatment they prefer, it is a much stronger statement on industrial democracy than many realize. Under the Wagner Act, managers are proscribed from taking unilateral action on mandatory bargaining items. The act guarantees bilateral determination and assures that no employer will institute or make changes in work rules without the consent of those who will be affected by those rules. Many states have enacted Wagner-Act-like provisions for governing unionization and collective bargaining among public employees.[3]

As work organizations "democratize," they become constitutional systems with emphasis on self-government and justice. The collective bargaining agreement becomes an important instrument of self-government, and arbitration of disputes becomes a critical element in establishing a system of justice. Both serve as protections against arbitrary or capricious behavior by management.

Another view of collective bargaining is that it is part of the process that establishes "a web of rules" to govern the work place and work community.[4] Work rules come from a number of sources. Governments require certain health and safety provisions, nondescrimination, and minimum wages. In the educational sector, government establishes certification and licensing standards that control job opportunity. School boards are empowered to make policy about a number of issues, and many of the rules that affect teachers and other school employees are the direct result of actions taken by local boards of education. Many rules now emanate from the collective bargaining arena; that is, they are bilaterally determined and written into a labor agreement. These become the web of rules which represents a work culture and is an important expression of control in the work place.

GENERAL EFFECTS OF COLLECTIVE BARGAINING IN EDUCATIONAL SETTINGS

One of the outcomes of the growth of teachers' unions and collective bargaining is that the teaching force has been secularized. Well into the 1950s teachers were viewed as dedicated workers, consistently placing the welfare of students above their own and enduring difficult circumstances in order to inspire the acquisition of knowledge in students. Teaching was seen almost as a calling rather than a job. Today, many do not hold such lofty views.

Another general outcome of collective bargaining in public education has been that division between administrators and teachers has been highlighted. As late as the mid-1960s teachers and administrators belonged to the same national organization. In local districts teachers and administrators all belonged to local teachers' associations. As collective bargaining began to emerge, conflicts between administrators and teachers became more obvious and more difficult to reconcile within one organizational framework. Numerous organizations for administrators have developed, separate from teachers' organizations.

In the prebargaining era, administrators' salaries were often indexed to teachers' salary schedules. Administrators were placed first on a teacher salary schedule and then paid a wage that was the teaching salary plus a percentage. That practice has been almost entirely abandoned in all but the smallest school districts because it creates an apparent conflict between administrators' interests and the administrative "side" in the bargaining process. If administrators were dependent upon teachers' successes in the bargaining process to enhance their own incomes they might be less willing to take a hard stand in salary negotiations.

Related to collective bargaining and to the unionization of teachers has been the increasing professionalization and separation of administration. Education administration has become a separate job, not an extension of a teaching career. After World War II states began to move aggressively toward the establishment of separate certification and training standards for school administrators in the United States. This led to an administrative cadre trained with management concepts.

Another general outcome of collective bargaining has been the highlighting of governance conflict. Disputes among education professionals at various levels and differences between educators and boards of education have been aired in public. Teachers' unions take full page ads in newspapers decrying conditions they believe to be unfair or unfavorable. Unions sponsor candidates and lobby legislators. All these activities are public expressions of belief and desire. Newspapers cover the bargaining process and describe differences between those at the bargaining table. All of this has left the general public with a heightened awareness of conflict among individuals who have responsibility at various levels for education.

EFFECTS OF COLLECTIVE BARGAINING IN SCHOOL DISTRICTS

Collective bargaining has had a number of effects on school districts and school district management. One might be called the "institutionalization" of collective bargaining. As has been mentioned, most teachers belong to teachers' unions and are represented by those unions in deliberations with school districts over salaries and other conditions of service. Collective bargaining is a process that is anticipated and districts now budget and staff to satisfy the demand of collective bargaining. It has been estimated variously that the preparation for negotiations, conduct of negotiations, and administration of the contract consumes a sizeable amount of school district and teacher resources. Currently that amount is estimated at about $35 per pupil in personnel time and direct financial outlay for purchase services, legal counsel, or third party impasse resolution expenses.[5] A district of five thousand students could expect to commit nearly $175,000 annually to bargaining-related activities in personnel and direct cost expenditures.

Not only has collective bargaining generated sizeable personnel time costs and expenditure commitments of a school district but many individuals owe their livelihood to the institution of collective bargaining in education. Many districts hire staff relations or bargaining specialists whose job it is to organize and conduct the district negotiations. In many towns across America there are local attorneys who specialize in negotiations for boards of education and a substantial amount of their practice is devoted to conducting this business. A half dozen information services have sprung up to support the bargaining specialists by providing everything from background information and comparative settlements to contract language and court awards relating to employment practice.

Although collective bargaining in education is greatly concerned with wage bargains, there are three pieces of evidence that suggest that collective bargaining has had relatively little influence on teachers' salaries:

1. Wage differences between bargaining and nonbargaining districts are small when district wealth and other contextual factors are controlled.
2. Teachers' wages have not increased relative to other workers during the period of rapid unionization and collective bargaining development in schools.
3. The share of district revenues going to teachers' wages has declined during the same period.

A large number of studies have examined the effects of collective bargaining on teachers' salaries. Some studies have focused on individual salaries,[6] most have analyzed average or scheduled salaries in districts,[7] and a few have examined regional or state impacts on teachers' salaries.[8] Although a few studies show effects of 20 percent or more, most researchers have found salary effects of collective bargaining to be much lower, typically in a range of zero to eight percent.

The size of the effect seems to be dependent on the unit of analysis and choice of salary measures. Studies of individual teacher's salaries have consistently shown higher effects than district or state salary aggregate analyses. Effects on beginning salaries have been consistently low, often approaching zero.

Attempts to measure the direct effects of collective bargaining on salaries have been plagued with some very difficult methodological problems. For one thing, wages in one district are greatly influenced by wages in adjacent districts. Teacher wages are also sensitive to wages in other sectors, particularly those in other public agencies. Finally, teachers' wages are influenced by a number of non-wage contextual factors such as teacher supply and demand, district income, and patron expectations. No fully satisfactory methodology exists to overcome all of these problems; thus, studies of collective bargaining salary effects must be interpreted cautiously.

Another approach to studying the salary effects of collective bargaining lies in cross-occupational wage study. Teachers are the most completely organized group of employees in the United States. If the unions had been successful in increasing teachers' wages through collective bargaining, teachers' wages should have increased relative to wages in less organized sectors of the economy. Comparisons of average teachers' wages with average or beginning wages in other professions and work groups do not support such a conclusion. Teachers have not made gains relative to other employees during the period of rapid unionization and collective bargaining development.[9]

An indicator of the fiscal impact of teachers' unions is in the relative share of district budgets that is devoted to teachers' salaries. In most districts, the share of the budget that goes to support teachers' salaries has been declining steadily for the last dozen years, which indicates that district budgets have grown more rapidly than teachers' salaries. Expenditures have been growing more rapidly for non-teacher salaries and nonsalary items than they have for teachers' salaries, hardly the budget direction that would be supported by a dominant teachers' union.

The general consensus among researchers is that collective bargaining has had a small positive effect on teacher salaries but that the effect has been less than the collective bargaining wage effects for the private sector, which are estimated to be between 15 and 25 percent.[10] Certainly collective bargaining has not led to a union raid on the public treasury as some had feared.

It would appear that school boards and administrators need not be concerned that budget priorities will be implicitly set in collective bargaining. Although they will be forced to defend resource allocation decisions, collective bargaining will not remove this important function from the arena of management and governance.

Although collective bargaining cannot be shown to have brought about significant changes in teachers' salaries, there are changes that are associated with bargaining. First, as bargaining relationships mature, an increasing number of items fall within the scope of bargaining. Studies have indicated that the number of items now included in contracts is significantly larger than the number of items that were included ten years ago.[11] This would seem to indicate that school districts and teachers' unions are turning more and more to collective bargaining as a primary mechanism for joint rule determination.

The reliance on collective bargaining as a way of establishing work rules may be accounted for in several ways. One is the shift in management thinking about collective bargaining over time. Education managers started out with a very hostile view of collective bargaining; they resisted all attempts to add items to the collective bargaining agenda. Over time school administrators developed familiarity with the process and became more comfortable with it. They also came to accept the process itself and its staying power. They then began to use collective bargaining more aggressively to meet their own policy objectives.[12] At this point collective bargaining began to resolve organizational problems and was used to develop legitimate organizational work rules.[13]

There are four major decision arenas in school districts: a public (or political) arena, a professional-bureaucratic arena, a labor relations arena, and a private arena. Each of these arenas attracts a different set of actors and has a different set of rules for the exercise of influence. In the public arena boards of education are influential by virtue of their elective representative status, the rules of the game are political, and pluralism prevails. Hierarchical position in the organization provides important leverage in the professional-bureaucratic arena. Decisions in this arena are made on the basis of technical expertise and positional power; administrators tend to be most powerful in this arena. Collective bargaining is part of the labor relations arena. This is the arena in which teachers can exhibit the greatest power by attempting to push decisions they wish to influence.[14]

As administrators use collective bargaining as a vehicle to pursue policy objectives, to solve organizational problems, or to develop work rules that will be more acceptable to teachers, the number of items on the bargaining agenda will increase, as will the scope of bargaining. If unions are successful in shifting decisions to the labor relations arena, where they can have greater voice, the importance of collective bargaining will grow, and the proportion of rules that are bilaterally determined will expand.

EFFECTS OF COLLECTIVE BARGAINING IN SCHOOLS

Partly because collective bargaining takes place at the district level, most attention has been given to districtwide impacts. The labor agreement is assumed to have uniform impact on all district personnel. In recent years there has been a growing awareness that collective bargaining has significant and selective influence on the school.[15]

The school is the primary work place for education. It is the place where teachers go to do their work and it is the place where students report to be educated. Within the school there are a number of issues raised by collective bargaining and several loci of impact to be examined. For example, administrative work and authority within the school are likely to be changed by collective bargaining.

Work rules developed at the district level through collective bargaining and other mechanisms have their primary impact in schools. It is in schools that teachers choose to accept or reject those rules. The possibility must be explored that negotiated work rules may be redefined at the work place.

Collective bargaining may also influence the way teachers work and the way teachers think about their work. Teachers are the primary workforce in schools, and the way they conceive and execute their work becomes the essential determinant of the success of the school enterprise.

The chief administrator of a school is the principal. Like other site managers, the principal's job is in part defined by district expectations and in part defined by the needs and expectations of those in the school. The work of a principal is affected in five ways by collective bargaining. First, the labor agreement sets forth rules that determine rights and duties of principals. Second, principals' actions are under constant scrutiny by union representatives in the building. Third, unions may, in the form of a building representative, insert a second formal leader into the school. Fourth, because most collective bargaining agreements contain grievance procedures, principals' actions may be formally challenged. Finally, collective bargaining can change informal as well as formal work relationships between principals and teachers.

Principals are called upon to administer a labor agreement that was probably negotiated without their involvement. They are under considerable pressure from the district to follow strict, literal interpretation of terms and to administer the agreement uniformly in all schools. Conscious of the dangers in diverse administration, districts often seek to centralize and standardize contract administration.[16] On the other hand, teachers will press to have the agreement interpreted in a way that takes particular school conditions into account. The ability of principals to manage these contradictory expectations is a major determinant of their effectiveness.

Some contend that the principals have lost necessary authority because of collective bargaining and are therefore unable to serve effectively. The evidence indicates that principals have lost formal authority under collective bargaining and teachers have gained power. There is no evidence, however, that unions and collective bargaining deprive managers of essential power. Comprehensive research for the private sector shows that collective bargaining has a weakening effect on poor managers but certainly does not weaken, and perhaps strengthens, good managers.[17] Effective managers are able to develop constructive relationships with shop stewards; they anticipate consequences of actions, reducing dysfunctional conflict and challenges by union representatives.

There are reasons to believe that good principals can prosper under collective bargaining as well. It has been shown that the contract is used by effective principals to improve management practices and to involve teachers more in school decisions.[18] The union practice of naming building representatives for each school provides principals with a designated conduit for teacher concerns and a way to test proposed changes informally. Effective principals have been shown to nurture a collaborative relationship with building representatives.[19]

Under collective bargaining principals are accountable for their actions to their subordinates through the grievance process. Grievances present several problems for principals. First, teachers can use them for strategic purposes to gain concessions from the principal. Each grievance filed requires certain formal actions to be taken and considerable paperwork, regardless of the outcome. Teachers can literally tie up a principal with grievance processing. Second, grievances become a matter of record, and involve superordinates in the district structure. Principals "look bad" if they have many grievances filed against them. Embarrassing questions may be asked. It is in the principal's interest to keep grievances down.

Principals can have considerable latitude when it comes to contract implementation. Within the same district there is likely to be great variation in the way rules are treated and adhered to among schools. Principals apparently can negotiate rule accommodations with their faculty and union representatives. In industrial relations the process by which individuals in the workplace modify rules to make them more suitable and more consistent with the needs of the individual setting is called "fractional bargaining." In order for rules to be legitimate they must relate to the mission of the organization. In terms of the school, that means that teachers judge work rules, regardless of the source, in terms of their consistency with the perceived mission of their school. If the rules contribute or are necessary to the establishment of an effective instructional program they are judged legitimate. If they appear to retard those processes or make it difficult for teachers and principals to go about their work, they are judged illegitimate and become candidates for local modification. Principals, it seems, will bend or alter rules to make them more consistent with the needs of their schools.

Little is known about criteria used for fractional bargaining in schools. There are probably some rules that are out of bounds to principals and that will not be modified even though they are not consistent with the direction and purpose of the schools. Modification of the rules may be related to two factors. First, rules communicate trust as well as direction. Prescriptive or proscriptive rules suggest to people that they can't be trusted. Detailed rules about the operation of work convey distrust. To the extent that principals are sensitive to this, they may intervene to convert rules from prescriptive to discretionary. They may treat rules as guidelines, as suggestions, which may make sense under many circumstances.[20]

Another reason principals may intervene in the enforcement or implementation of contractual rules is to increase their credibility so that certain important school functions can be carried forward. Fox talked about the difference between social exchanges and economic or market exchanges in social systems. He points out that individuals exchange property and property rights to gain the things they need or want. There are two basic kinds of exchanges that people engage in for this purpose. First is a social exchange. This is an asymmetric process in which one party does something now for another party in the expectation that in the future the favor will be repaid. Because of the unspecified nature of the exchange, and the time delay in its completion, this type of exchange is used only under circumstances of trust. Thus, a principal may arrange coverage for a teacher who needs to make a trip to the bank or to the dentist during the contract day with the expectation that that teacher will be more helpful or cooperative in some of the programs that the principal wishes to push forward in the school building. In a sense the rules themselves may become a subject of exchange and their enforcement or interpretation may be traded off for other values to make the school run more efficiently.

Where trust is low, exchanges become more formal. Certainly one outcome of collective bargaining has been the fact that work rules have become more explicit. This is an automatic result of the collective bargaining process. As negotiators attempt to develop enforceable work rules they try to account for the complexity in professional work. The rules themselves become much more involved and much more comprehensive. Examples of this are the definition of the contract day, provision for break times, and other items that have been incorporated in the work environment of teachers. That is not to say that these developments are necessarily bad. If nothing else, they force those in school systems to think hard about the nature of teaching.

To the degree that rules become more explicit, they tend to communicate minimum standards of performance. School districts cannot operate efficiently on minimum acceptable performance standards, and this can be especially destructive in the teaching environment. To some degree the effect has been the increasing rationalization of the work place. There are more rules, the rules are more explicit, most of the rules emanate from a central source, and they allow for less and less leeway. Save for the practice of fractional bargaining, teachers find themselves being increasingly locked in a web of rules that completely defines their work day and work procedures.

The attempts to explicitly define teachers' work has implications for principals' work. For one thing, principals may be limited in their ability to assign extra duties or to schedule after-school meetings. Second, it means that principals must judge performance of teachers in terms of contractual performance requirements that may be less comprehensive and less rigorous than professional standards of good teaching practice.

THE EFFECTS OF COLLECTIVE BARGAINING ON THE TEACHING PROFESSION

Collective bargaining places countervailing pressures on teaching. On the one hand, it gives teachers a greater voice in determining working conditions. Under collective bargaining, teachers have shortened their contract day and their teaching day, reduced non-teaching duties, limited class size, and gained preparation time. Teachers have also gained job protections and procedural guarantees. On the other hand, collective bargaining has led to more explicit regulation of teachers and teaching work. Thus teaching has become more rationalized.

The rationalization of work has its origin in the thinking of Max Weber, the German sociologist, and Frederick Winslow Taylor, the American industrial engineer. In scientific management there is an overriding notion that work must be standardized and carefully planned; it is the responsibility of central authorities to define and plan the work. It is the obligation of the worker to carry out those plans. The degree to which work organization and work execution are unified is important in thinking about work. The hallmark of scientific management was the complete separation of the organization and the execution of work. To the extent that collective bargaining reinforces notions of central rule making and explicit work rules it reinforces this separation. The separation of organization and execution in work, however, runs contrary to much thinking about professions and professional work.

Mitchell and Kerchner have suggested that collective bargaining and labor relations policy help shape our view of teaching as "labor." They contend that collective bargaining tends to support the rationalization of work (work is preplanned and routinized instead of adaptive and flexible) and the use of direct inspection as a method of oversight. These are views that characterize work as labor rather than work as a profession, craft, or art.[21] This suggests that there may be need for extensive modification of labor relations policies in school districts if they are to support the development of professionals in the school environment.

CONCLUSION

This paper has examined aspects of collective bargaining as it influences the behavior of managers and policymakers in school systems. Three things can be said about the effects of collective bargaining: they are not as drastic as many projected they would be, some appear quite positive, and some are worrisome.

There have always been two strong reservations about collective bargaining among managers and policymakers. Those are that unions will loot the public treasury in quest of higher salaries and that managers will lose the ability to manage. Neither fear seems to have been realized. Salary gains to teachers through collective bargaining have been modest and there is no evidence that teachers' unions have successfully pursued a bargaining agenda that has distorted district resource allocation practices. School managers can still manage under provisions of collective bargaining. Principals, even with the strongest union, have plenty of power to manage effectively. In fact, the addition of labor relations expectations has seemingly made some administrators more effective.

As a result of collective bargaining, teachers have gained greater voice in many district and school decisions. School districts and schools are more democratic organizations as a result, and teachers have the mechanism to press their concerns. They have also acquired job protections and protection against arbitrary and capricious administrative actions through grievance enactments. Unions have improved communication between administrators in many cases. These are all positive developments.

Worrisome, however, is the increasing detail of contracts and the degree to which teaching is increasingly being regulated by explicit work rules. The burden of extensive rules is great in a professional organization. They signal distrust of and lack of confidence in teachers. They may formalize administrator-teacher relationships and lead to a view of teaching as labor.

NOTES

1. Tannenbaum has pointed out that because unions are dependent organizations they will always take their cues from organizational conditions. See Arnold S. Tannenbaum, "Unions," in James March, ed., *Handbook of Organizations* (Chicago: Rand McNally and Co., 1965). For a more complete discussion of the causes of unionism among teachers see Anthony M. Cresswell and Michael J. Murphy, *Teachers, Unions and Collective Bargaining in Public Education* (Berkeley, California: McCutchan Publishing Corp., 1980), chapters 3 and 4.
2. This view is forcefully represented in Philip Selznick's *Law, Society and Industrial Justice* (Russell Sage Foundation, 1969). Freeman and Medoff seem to support the view that an important union effect is a more democratic and responsive workplace. See Richard B. Freeman and James L. Medoff, "The Two Faces of Unionism," *The Public Interest* 57 (Fall 1979), pp. 69–93.
3. For an examination of the consequence of mandatory bargaining of school board decision prerogatives see Diana D. Halpenny, "The Impact of Collective Bargaining on California Education Code Laws Governing Teacher Tenure, Evaluations, and Dismissal," *Pacific Law Journal* (April 1980), pp. 799–820.
4. This view is credited to John Dunlop who first proposed it in *Industrial Relations Systems* (New York: McGraw-Hill, 1958) as a way of cross-industrial and cross-national study of employment relations systems.
5. See Michael J. Murphy, "Employment Relations and Collective Bargaining," in Guilbert C. Hentschke, ed., *School Business Administration: A Comparative Perspective* (in press).
6. Baugh and Stone's studies are a good example. They did an analysis of union membership, membership in a collective bargaining unit, and salaries earned among teachers in a large national data base. See William H. Baugh and Joe A. Stone, "Teachers, Unions, and Wages in the 1970's: Unionism Now Pays," *Industrial and Labor Relations Review* 35 (April 1982), pp. 368–376. See also Jay G. Chambers, "An Analysis of Resource Allocation in Public School Districts," *Public Finance Quarterly* 6 (April 1978), pp. 131–160; and Alexander B. Holmes, "Effects of Union Activity on Teachers' Earnings," *Industrial Relations* 15 (October 1976) pp. 328–332.
7. Studies of this type are too numerous to list here. There are some excellent summaries available, however. See David B. Lipsky, "The Effect of Collective Bargaining on Teacher Pay: A Review of the Evidence," *Educational Administration Quarterly* 18 (Winter 1982), pp. 14–42. See also Anthony M. Cresswell and Michael J. Murphy, *Teachers, Unions and Collective Bargaining in Education*, pp. 447–452; and Anthony M. Cresswell and Fay Spargo, *Impacts of Collective Bargaining Policy in Elementary and Secondary Education: A Review of Research and Methodology; Recommendations for New Research* (Education Commission of the States, August 1980).
8. See Alan L. Gustman and Martin Segal, "Teachers' Salary Structures—Some Analytical and Empirical Aspects of the Impact of Collective Bargaining," Industrial Relations Research Association, *Proceedings of the Thirtieth Annual Meeting, 1977* (Madison, WI: 1978); and Anthony M. Cresswell, et

al., "Impacting State Labor Relations and School Finance Policies on Educational Resource Allocation" (paper presented at the American Educational Research Association Annual Meeting, 1978).

9. See Michael J. Murphy, "One More Time: Do Teachers' Unions Raise Teachers' Salaries?" (paper presented at the National Conference of Professors of Educational Administration in Seattle, Washington, August 1981).

10. Lipsky, "The Effect of Collective Bargaining on Teacher Pay."

11. See Lorraine McDonnell and Anthony Pascal, *Organized Teachers in American Schools* (Santa Monica, CA: Rand Corporation, 1979).

12. Mitchell and Kerchner, who have studied this phenomenon, suggest that administrators ultimately come to see collective bargaining in terms of policy development and become aggressive in pressing their own agenda in negotiations. Douglas E. Mitchell, Charles T. Kerchner, Wayne Erck, and Gabrielle Pryor, "The Impact of Collective Bargaining on School Management and Policy," *American Journal of Education* (February 1981).

13. Walton and McKersie have noted that bargaining serves not only to distribute scarce resources but also to facilitate organizational problem solving. This they refer to as "integrative" bargaining. See Richard E. Walton and Robert B. McKersie, *A Behavioral Theory of Labor Negotiations* (New York: McGraw-Hill, 1965). Freeman and Medoff also stress the organizational problem-solving potential in unionization and collective bargaining. See Freeman and Medoff, "The Two Faces of Unionism."

14. For a more complete discussion of these arenas see Cresswell and Murphy, *Teachers, Unions and Collective Bargaining in Public Education*, chapter 6.

15. McDonnell and Pascal have concluded that the contract has the greatest nonbudgetary influence at the school level. See McDonnell and Pascal, *Organized Teachers in American Schools*. Johnson and others have found great variability in the way contract provisions are implemented in schools. See Susan Moore Johnson, *Teacher Unions in Schools* (Philadelphia: Temple University Press, 1984).

16. Mitchell, et al., McDonnell and Pascal, and Johnson have all found these pressures in their research.

17. Sumner H. Slichter, James J. Healy, and E. Robert Livernash, *The Impact of Collective Bargaining on Management* (Washington, D.C.: The Brookings Institution, 1960).

18. McDonnell and Pascal, *Organized Teachers in American Schools*, p. 81.

19. See Neil Ellman, "Union-Administration Cooperation in the Public Schools of New York City," unpublished dissertation, Teachers College, Columbia University, 1972. See also Johnson, *Teacher Unions in Schools*; and Alan M. Glassman and James A. Belasco, "The Chapter Chairman and School Grievances," in Anthony M. Cresswell and Michael J. Murphy, eds., *Education and Collective Bargaining* (Berkeley, CA: McCutchan Publishing Corp., 1976).

20. Fox has discussed the relationship between rules and trust. See Alan Fox, *Beyond Contract: Work, Power and Trust Relations* (London: Faber and Faber, Ltd., 1974).

21. See Douglas E. Mitchell and Charles T. Kerchner, "Labor Relations and Teacher Policy," in Lee S. Schulman and Gary Sykes, eds., *Handbook of Teaching and Policy* (New York: Longman, 1983).

GUILBERT C. HENTSCHKE

Emerging Roles of School District Administrators: Implications for Planning, Budgeting, and Management

School district administrators are defining new roles for themselves, adding to their more traditional role. The traditional role is characteristic of purely "public sector" managers, whereas the emerging roles are more characteristic of purely "private sector" managers (both the for-profit and not-for-profit private sectors).[1] A primary cause of the development of the new role is that school administrators are beginning to pursue revenue-generating opportunities via private sector models due to the limits of the public sector model. The traditional role, the new role, and the implications of their mutual presence in school districts are examined in this paper.

SCHOOL ADMINISTRATORS AS CHARACTERISTICALLY PUBLIC SECTOR MANAGERS

The term "public sector" has a variety of meanings. In the context of schools its meaning is best captured by Niskanen's description of the typical public enterprise or "bureau."[2] School districts provide a certain set of activities in exchange for a lump sum budget appropriation. The demands of sponsors—revenue providers at the local, state, and federal levels—as revealed for public schooling are related to those of their constituents as revealed through the political process. However, the demands of the populace for schooling are never fully revealed to administrators of a school district because people do not decide what will be offered in schools by choosing among alternatives. Rather, through budget votes, elections, and lobbying, they attempt to influence the decisions of school administrators. School administrators may, of course, appeal to their sponsors' constituents in an attempt to increase the demand for educational services.

Characteristic behavior of administrators in school districts is to maximize their budgets. Such behavior is due to the incentives facing them. They, like the rest of us, seek to maximize personal utility. This implies budget maximization for two reasons: rationality and survival. Among the items desired by the school administrator are sal-

Guilbert C. Hentschke is acting dean, Graduate School of Education, University of Rochester.

ary, perquisites of office, public reputation, power, schooling outcomes, patronage, and ease of managing the school district. All of these are related to the total budget of the school district.

The survival argument also suggests why school administrators seek to maximize budgets. The two groups of people that significantly influence the tenure of school administrators are the employees of the school district and its sponsors. To varying degrees, individuals employed by the district also desire budget maximization and influence the school administration to seek increased budgets. As Niskanen points out, for all public bureaus, "(employees) can be cooperative, responsive, and efficient. Or they can deny information to the (school administrator), undermining his directive, and embarrass him before the (public). Their behavior depends on their perceived rewards of employment in the (school district)."[3] The administrator who seeks operating efficiencies without budget increases will have difficulty "buying the cooperation" of employees. Efficiencies usually occur when the rate of increase in pressures for spending are constrained by budgets that are not expanding as rapidly.[4]

This does not mean that school administrators' interests are other than "professional." Most school administrators, by either predisposition or training, undoubtedly try to serve their perception of the public interest.

Sponsors also have an interest in school district budget maximization, although their reasons are less obvious. Parents' interests in higher spending are a major force for increased budgets, despite the fact that parents of school age children constitute a declining proportion of taxpayers in many school districts and taxpayer groups are becoming more successful in defeating budget increases. School boards and state legislatures often lack the time, the information, and the staff necessary to evaluate budgets. "At every stage in a multistage review process, the review officers are dependent on the bureaucrat to make a forceful case for his proposed budget."[5]

Two forces work against school district budget maximizaton. First, for sponsors, education is but one of many services competing for their scarce resources. Second, as sponsors allocate more resources to school districts, they have to expend additional resources to monitor and control school administrators to insure that their educational preferences, not district administrators' preferences, are being pursued. The greater the incremental increase in budgets, the less likely that sponsor preferences will be pursued. The details of the contest over appropriation and control are played out differently in school districts and states. The wide variety of mechanisms to appropriate resources— aid formulas, budget votes, grant procedures—vary, but the fundamental contest exists in all cases. The challenge to the public manager is to maximize his total budget, then adjust his expenditures to live within the line item and overall budget constraints.

Increasingly in recent years the internally and externally imposed demands on school administrators for schooling services have increased more than budgets have increased.[6] Increased fiscal strain in school districts increases the utility to administrators of pursuing nontraditional sources of revenue. After years of seeking to extract as much as possible from public tax sources, school administrators are turning to non-public sources in pursuit of revenue. Increasingly the public school administrator is adopting behaviors of the purely private sector manager.

CHARACTERISTICS OF PRIVATE SECTOR MANAGERS

The purely private sector manager differs in fundamental ways from his public sector counterpart, especially in his relations with sponsors and those who consume his services (constituents, clients, or consumers). The purely private sector manager has much greater discretion over the services he produces. He faces different incentives.

His measure of success is not budget maximization, but maximization of the stream of net revenues discounted over future periods.[7] He has incentives to maximize net revenues because the more net revenue he can generate, the greater his ability to pursue his preferences. He pursues efficiencies as part of his effort to maximize discounted cash flows. He will reduce expenditures in ways that do not communicate to the consumer a curtailment of services.

The private sector manager does not face the same kind of scrutiny from sponsors as his public sector counterpart. Private sector sponsors rely less on expensive monitoring mechanisms in order to insure administrative compliance with their preferences. Rather, they may easily shift the purchase of services from one provider to another. Likewise, when particular programs do not generate desired net revenues, purely private managers are more free to discontinue some services and to initiate those with a greater chance of generating positive cash flow.

The limits imposed on private sector managers are those of the marketplace. The challenge facing purely private managers is to develop missions and services, price them, and find markets for them so that they produce a stream of net revenues.

EVOLUTIONARY CHANGES IN THE WAY SCHOOLS SEEK AND EXPEND RESOURCES

The public manager and private manager stereotypes are distinguished from each other primarily in terms of the manner in which they seek and expend monetary and non-monetary resources. The goal of this section is to outline the major ways in which public school administrators increasingly are assuming private manager roles by seeking and expending resources in new ways.

Traditionally, school district administrators pursued only monetary resources, and pursued these almost entirely through intergovernmental transfer mechanisms and direct taxation. On the expenditure side, they have been increasingly constrained by spending rules laid down by governmental resource providers. Controls take the form of regulations that stipulate what resources are to be used, how they are to be organized, and what results are to be produced.[8] They are backed up by sanctions of varying kinds to insure nominal compliance.[9]

The purely public model of public school administration is increasingly an incomplete description of the major ways in which school district administrators raise and expend resources. In addition to the traditional public role of lobbying for appropriations, three additional methods more characteristic of private sector managers are being used in public school administration: pursuing sales with individuals and organizations; pursuing donations; and contracting for services, including instruction, when it appears to maximize net revenues. Although there are many specific instances of each type of behavior, their overall quantity and impact are not yet clear. There is, however, a sense that the trend is toward greater reliance on these emerging mechanisms.

Selling to Consumer Markets

As school district administrators perceive more and more fiscal strain within the context of their traditional public sector role, they are increasingly looking at the opportunities to sell goods and services in order to generate net revenues. They sell their district's goods and services to non-student markets, to student markets outside of the district, and to student markets already served by the district. For example, they are selling traditional K-12 educational services to new markets, such as students residing outside the district boundaries. They are selling nontraditional educational services to new markets, as is the case with adult education. And they are selling space to other providers of educational services, such as college extension programs and day care programs.[10]

The sale of instructional services and goods provides a greater variety of options to school district administrators. Some school districts are selling transportation, food, computer, vehicle maintenance, attendance, accounting, and test scoring services. Schools and classrooms are being leased to a variety of tenants. Even playing fields and locker rooms are being leased to professional sports teams for pre-season practice. Rural districts lease some of their land to farmers. Other districts have generated revenue by the selective harvesting of trees. Some districts have sold their gas and mineral rights. At least one rural school district sells water from its well. Districts run ''thrift shops'' to sell off surplus or obsolete school equipment or supplies. Some hold auctions to achieve the same end.[11]

School districts have for years sold the use of their excess cash to local banks to generate interest revenue. Recently, some districts have banded together and organized separate nonprofit organizations to achieve scale economies and to gain more freedom to pursue greater revenues through this mechanism.[12]

In all of the above activities the school district as agent sells its goods and services to clients other than K-12 students attending district schools. District administrators also sell access to their students to other purveyors of goods and services. Districts sell advertising space in school publications. Various concessions are offered to business for a fee, such as student pictures, vending machines, school rings, sports equipment, and clothing. Districts also sell directly to their student markets in the form of student fees for elective, nonmandated services such as swimming and driver education. In some states districts are charging annual textbook rental fees, locker maintenance fees, towel rental fees, student parking fees, and musical instrument rental fees. In other states schools charge a fee for elective courses.[13]

Pursuing Donor Markets

Donor markets differ from consumer markets only in the degree to which money is inherent in the transaction. Both instances are predicated on exchanges between two parties where each feels that what is received is of greater value than what has been given up.[14]

What is "sold" to donors is the opportunity to provide resources to improve schools in ways desired by the donors. School district administrators make it possible for donors to identify services they want performed in schools and, when administrator and donor preferences match, to cause those services to be provided. The contribution may be monetary or nonmonetary. Nonmonetary contributions include goods and services.

School administrators are pursuing donors through various strategies. Predominant among these are newly created, private nonprofit organizations that are devoted solely to "improving" or "benefiting" public schools. Over the last few years these voluntary nonprofit structures (sometimes called "public education funds") have been formed in dozens of major cities across the country, including San Francisco, Dallas, Los Angeles, Rochester (N.Y.), Oakland, Tucson, Wilmington, Charleston, Raleigh, Decatur, Cleveland, Pittsburgh, Paterson (N.J.), and Washington, D.C.[15] These organizations are themselves a means for individuals to contribute their services to schools. Individual donors are contributing many hours of their time to these organizations in an effort to help them grow and prosper.

In almost all cases the programs of these organizations are meant to supplement, not replicate, existing services in the school district. "Enrichment" goods and services provided through these organizations are diverse and each benefits only a small percentage of students in the school district. In San Francisco, for example, donors have contributed money to fund oral language skills, wordless picture books, a storytellers' club, manual typewriters, a life science program, creative writing, microscopes, microcomputers, wildlife study, creative geometry, competitive speaking, a weather station, humanists in the school, Hispanic culture enrichment, and after-school instrumental music instruction.[16] These "mini-grant programs" award donor dollars to school employees (largely teachers) who develop small-scale, competitive proposals.

In another type of program called "adopt a school" or "school partnerships," organizations in the community are matched with schools. School administrators negotiate with managers in participating organizations to supply those goods and services that they wish to contribute. One such major partnership is in the Pittsburgh schools.

In these and other programs, donors enter into an exchange. In return for donations, donors may receive personal satisfaction, public recognition, and, often, tax write-offs.

Contracting for Services

The third departure from the traditional "public" role of the public school administrator is currently least in evidence, yet portends the greatest potential change in the role of the school district administrator: contracting for instruction. For many years schools district administrators have routinely contracted for noninstructional services as an alternative to direct provision, and currently private contractors provide a wide array of noninstructional services to school districts, most commonly for transportation, food, and custodial services. Some districts also contract for certain personnel functions, security services, energy management, data processing, accounting, and cash management.[17]

With very few exceptions school administrators have assumed that a prohibition exists against contracting for instructional services.[18] Such a prohibition may be real or imagined. Where that prohibition does not exist, school district administrators are beginning to contract with private organizations to provide instructional services heretofore provided by district-employed teachers.

Limited experience with district contracting for instruction suggests that the results may be similar to the more common instances where municipal and regional governments have contracted out some of their services. Comparative analyses of municipal contracting with direct provision suggest that, with notable exception, costs tend to be somewhat less and quality of services is comparable or better.[19]

Recent performance of one organization, Ombudsman Educational Services, Ltd., may well be indicative of general relationships. School administrators in about 40 school districts in Illinois and Arizona are contracting with Ombudsman, a private for-profit organization, to provide instructional services to some of their high school students who have difficulty in traditional classroom settings and are not likely to complete high school if they remain in the traditional classroom. The program is structured with a pupil-teacher ratio of about 5 to 1 as well as extensive exposure to microcomputers. Ombudsman charges the Illinois districts about $2,200 tuition per pupil—a fee that is about $500 less than the state average per student expenditure for public elementary and secondary schools. In Arizona:

All of the larger (client) school districts . . . offer in-house alternative programs for students who are not succeeding. Costs for these programs are at least twice the cost of the Ombudsman program. Therefore the districts have been extremely positive about referring students to Ombudsman.[20]

Ombudsman achieves lower costs in three interrelated ways. First, while its professional staff are all state-certified, they are paid on the average less than their counterparts in the public schools. Second, all school time is allocated to instructional tasks, and services for any student are limited to about three hours per day. Third, up to a half of all student work takes place on microcomputers with Autotutor software.[21]

The data on school district contracting for instruction are still inconclusive. The degree to which Ombudsman is "typical" is not clear. However, relatively lower unit labor costs and greater capital intensity is characteristic of for-profit firms where comparative studies have been conducted.[22]

DIFFERENCES BETWEEN THE TRADITIONAL AND EMERGING ROLES

Of the various distinctions between the "public" and "private" roles, five have the greatest long-run implications for changing the role of the public school administrator and, hence, for changing public schools:

1. Providing services solely to school age children in the district's attendance area versus

providing instructional and noninstructional services to other organizations and to non-traditional students.

2. Providing all services free of charge versus attaching prices to selected services.
3. Striving to provide identical services to all children versus promoting intradistrict differences in services and educational opportunities among similar types of students.
4. Providing instructional services almost entirely through hired employees versus contracting for some instructional services.
5. Arguing for revenues by relying on the threefold rationale of imminent educational problems resulting from elimination or underfunding of programs, unmet needs of children, and civic responsibility of taxpayers to support public schools versus selling, i.e., convincing nongovernmental organizations and individuals to purchase or donate goods, services, and money by emphasizing the high quality, competitive price, and civic-worthiness of school services.

All five of these distinctions are variations and manifestations of one underlying theme—a theme reflecting movement from the school administrator as the implementor of state, federal, and contractual mandates within legislatively determined revenue limits to the inventor of and money raiser for locally determined initiatives. Much of the difference between the two types of management behaviors is tied to the way in which the school administrator addresses relationships between production levels and associated costs and revenues. Production levels assume a given technology and a variable volume of service. Costs associated with that service are assumed to include both fixed cost components and variable cost components. The total cost of producing a given level of service is the sum of fixed and variable costs.

These relationships between production levels and costs (portrayed graphically in Figure 1) are generally alike for both types of managers, but here the similarity ends. The purely private manager evaluates markets, then sets prices and production levels to make acceptable net revenues. The purely public manager takes revenues and production levels as givens, then modifies technology in order to break even.

To make reasonably acceptable decisions, the purely private manager seeks to measure changes in the costs of particular items in relation to various kinds of changes in

FIGURE 1
Production-Cost Relationships, All Sectors

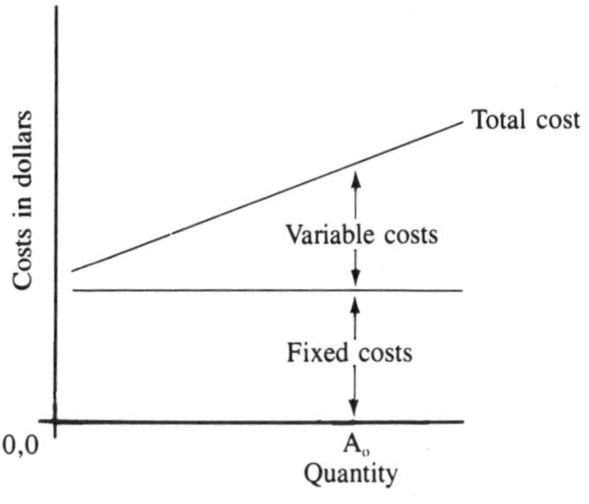

FIGURE 2
Private Sector Response to Cost-Production Relationships

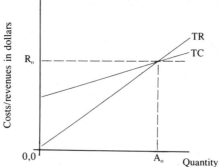

Given: Production-cost relationships.
Modify: Prices ($> R_o/A_o$).
Production levels (A_o) such that net revenues are realized ($TR > TC$).

business activity. The purpose of this estimation step is to isolate incremental costs for any given decision. The second step entails measuring relationships between total costs, rates of production of service, and total revenues. Purely private managers derive the great bulk of revenue to pay for a service from direct sales of the service to clients; they seek to set prices so that the revenues pay for all of the variable costs associated with one unit of service plus some contribution to the fixed costs. They seek to generate profit by producing beyond the break-even point where total revenues (TR) exceed total costs (TC). (See Figure 2.) Purely private managers estimate costs, demand and production levels, and enter production when the likelihood of generating net revenues sufficiently offsets the risks inherent in entering production. In determining the relationship between prices and production levels they estimate consumer behavior under different prices.

The purely public manager, in contrast, gets a lump sum budget appropriation (total revenue in Figure 3), may not charge any price, and does not determine production levels. Both Ro (price) and Ao (production level) are given. The purely public manager (such as a school district administrator) behaves as a budget maximizer, often asking for more revenue than the sponsor is willing to provide. When this occurs, total anticipated revenues exceed total estimated costs, and the purely public manager must decide how to adjust fixed and variable costs in such a way as to match expenditures and revenues (to make Ao and Ro intersect). In pure form the public sector manager exercises judgement over production—cost relationships in response to given revenues and production levels—whereas the purely private sector manager exercises more discretion over prices and production levels given production-cost relationships.

IMPLICATIONS FOR PUBLIC SCHOOL ADMINISTRATORS

To the degree that the "private" role of school administrators grows relative to their traditional public role, the job will likely become more complex, and additional criteria

FIGURE 3
Public Sector Response to Production-Cost Relationships

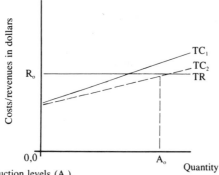

Given: Production levels (A$_o$).
Total revenue (TR).
Modify: Production-cost relationships such that total cost equals total revenue.

will emerge against which to evaluate administrative behavior. The implications of the differences described above are still unclear. Limited data suggest that the emerging private sector roles of school administrators will increase their rights and responsibilities and, hence, their opportunities to improve schooling. The local political environment in which they work will likely strengthen, and the criteria for evaluating the appropriateness of the services offered by the school district will be redefined.

Increased Administrative Control

The purely public model of school administrator is one largely of carrying out legally and contractually mandated services to legally and contractually defined clients. The purely public nature of school district administration is one of operational control, that is, ensuring that predetermined activities are carried out as intended. Traditionally, school administrators exercise little managerial control (determining those activities that best achieve predetermined objectives) and have even less control over strategic decisions (determining objectives).

With the emergence of the "private" role, school administrators will gain some greater control over the objectives they wish to pursue and the activities they wish to implement. As indicated earlier, administrators are already doing things to "enrich" the basic mission of public schools.

Although the new resources obtained from sales and donations have fewer strings tied to them, they are subject to some constraints. Net sales revenue usually is applied to the indirect costs associated with producing the service. With the inherent flexibility associated with developing indirect charge rates, district administrators use net revenues to reduce overhead, freeing up money for other uses. Donor resources are constrained in that school administrator and donor preferences have to be similar in order to effect the exchange. These resources are, by definition, more valued by the administrator because he or she is not required to pursue them.

The impact on control of curriculum follows from the general assumptions about control. To the extent that enrichment activities are interjected into the existing school program, they become part of (and indistinguishable from) the existing school program. School administrators have greater control over the selection of these enrichment activities and thereby have gained some measure of additional control over their schools.

The primary limit to contracting for instruction, other than legal restrictions and cultural prohibitions, will be the absence of suppliers for some years. Firms that have emerged in the last several years seem to be thriving and growing, but their share of the market is still small.[23]

Increased Local Support

The three types of private role activities are likely to increase political support for schools. The net impact is still unclear because some of the forces may be self-cancelling to a degree. However, research on voter behavior suggests that "yes" voting on school budgets is a positive function of familiarity with and involvement in schools.[24] Each of the private roles involves the community more extensively, even if only in increasing the number of buyers and sellers who transact business with the school district. Perhaps one of the most effective means to maximize budgets on the "public side" is to pursue emerging markets on the "private side," because the public and private markets overlap to a great extent.

The data are still not in on this issue, however. The opposite outcome can be argued with at least some conviction: provided with public and private conduits for schools, individuals will support the private (largely philanthropic) conduits at the expense of the public conduits in part because they can exert greater control over the curricula.

Redefinition of Equity

One of the most pervasive norms of public education is that children who have equivalent educational needs and abilities should be treated equally. The norm is embodied in state and federal laws, is referenced in court cases, and is evident in school district programming. As school administrators have translated that norm into curricular programming, "equal treatment" became "identical treatment" on the assumption that within any educational classification of children, each child should have access to identical, not merely equivalent, educational opportunities.

Increasingly, however, administrators are encouraging unique and special opportunities for individual classes of children or for children in a particular school. Certainly much of the donor activity (mini-grants and school partnerships) points in this direction. A major corporation such as IBM or American Airlines adopts two schools in one district, while at the same time a "mom and pop" grocery or a beauty parlor adopts two other schools. Although it is not clear from these examples which schools, if any, are thereby more advanced, it is clear that the impact will be decidedly different from school to school. The prevailing rationale of this apparent modification in norm is that "having unique good things to sprinkle around is preferrable to having nothing in sufficient quantity to distribute uniformly throughout the district."

Intradistrict equity will likely only shift from "identical" to "roughly equivalent" because of the inherent political pressures for equity which are applicable at the school board level. Indeed, many of the initial donor activities have been deliberately targeted at those schools most in need. The interdistrict ramifications of the emerging private roles, however, are likely to exacerbate some current inequities and ameliorate others. Districts with easy access to extensive donor markets, all else equal, will capture more donor resources than those with less access. Although adequate comparative data are not available, urban districts with extensive business and nonprofit organization resources seem to have an extensive advantage over rural districts. When examined on a per pupil basis, however, this advantage is less clear.

SPECULATION ON FUTURE DIRECTIONS

The presumptions discussed here are that a small "purely private" role is being played by the public school administrator alongside the currently much larger "purely public" role and that the private role is increasing. If the second presumption is valid, that is, if school administrators find that their jobs have more and more private sector content, the question arises: how will public school districts be different in the future?

In all likelihood, school districts will be seen as "better," and as a corollary, school administrators will be seen as doing a "better" job. Why is this? The purely private sector role is voluntary on the part of the school district administrator. He or she will pursue it when, and only to the extent that, the anticipated benefits outweigh the costs. Benefits in this context can take all kinds of forms—increased local support, increased revenue, personal prestige, improved schooling opportunities, enhanced employee morale, and so on. The purely private role is one more solution strategy that school district administrators are adding to their repertoire. To reiterate the obvious, those private initiatives which are less likely to bear fruit are less likely to be tried. Private-like initiatives do not, however, automatically guarantee that the desired ends will be achieved. As in the "real" private sector, it is also likely that many private initiatives in school districts will fail, and that many more things have not yet been tried.

Another, perhaps more fundamental, outcome of the trend will be a change in the nature of inquiry about how organizational structures affect society's delivery of collective goods such as K-12 schooling. It may be that the distinction between purely public and purely private organizations is becoming less and less clear. In an era when governments own and manage convention centers, yacht clubs, and golf courses and where private (including for-profit) organizations run day care centers, schools, and health clinics, there is less and less credence to the argument that a particular good or service is the province of a particular economic sector. Several analysts have recently called attention to the growing diversity of ways in which nonschool municipal services are being provided and how managers in each of the three sectors of society pursue the advantages of managers in other sectors whenever it is feasible.[25] The premise is that markets (for sales and donations) and hierarchies (departments and bureaus) are alternatives to each other, and that managers choose on the basis of utility maximization regardless of sector location. Increasingly, public organizations pursue donations (like private nonprofits), and they pursue net revenues from sales (like nonprofits and for-profits); private organizations (both nonprofit and for-profits) pursue tax revenues; all organizations pursue all markets for resources wherever feasible.

NOTES

1. "Private sector" here includes both for-profit and not-for-profit private organizations. Major differences differentiate the two private sectors, but those differences are not germane to the arguments presented here.
2. William A. Niskanen, *Bureaucracy: Servant or Master?* (Great Britain: The Institute of Economic Affairs, 1973).
3. Niskanen, p. 24.
4. Guilbert C. Hentschke and John Yagielski, "School District Fiscal Strain: Implications for State and Federal Assistance," *Journal of Education Finance* 8 (Summer 1982), pp. 52–72.
5. Niskanen, p. 25.
6. Hentschke and Yagielski.
7. James T. Bennett and Manuel H. Johnson, *Better Government at Half the Price: Private Production of Public Services* (Ottawa, IL: Carolina House Publishers, Inc., 1981).
8. Guy Benveniste, "Devising Strategies for Change," *IFG Policy Notes* 3 (Fall 1982), pp. 3–4.
9. David Kirp, "Controls and Consequences," *IFG Policy Notes* 3 (Fall 1982), pp. 1–2.
10. Lionel R. Meno, *An Examination of the Types of Nontraditional Financing Methods and Their Present and Potential Impact on Public School Districts* (Ed.D. dissertation, University of Rochester, 1983).
11. Laura Loomis, "Feasibility Study of Alternative Funding Sources for the North Rose-Wolcott Central School District, Wolcott, NY," March 1984.
12. Pennsylvania School District Liquid Asset Fund, "Information Statement," February 24, 1982
13. Meno.
14. Burton Weisbrod, *The Voluntary Nonprofit Sector* (Lexington, Mass.: D.C. Heath and Co., 1977).
15. Information on these projects can be obtained through the Public Education Fund. Contact David Bergholz, c/o P.E.F., 600 Grant Street, Suite 4444, Pittsburgh, PA 15219.
16. Gladys S. Thatcher, *The San Francisco Education Fund: 1982–83 Annual Grants Report* (San Francisco: The Fund, 1983).
17. See Loomis.
18. Meno.
19. E.S. Savas, *Privatizing the Public Sector* (Chatham, N.J.: Chatham House Publishers, Inc., 1982).
20. Ombudsman Educational Services, Ltd., "Report of Operations of the Lake County Learning Community 1981–82 School Year," memo, May 19, 1982.
21. William Wilken, "Ombudsman Raises Achievement, Cuts Costs with Micro Technology," *School Cost Management* 1 (November 30, 1982), pp. 4–5, 8.
22. Robert W. Poole, *Cutting Back City Hall* (New York: Universe Books, 1979).
23. Data on growth of these organizations are difficult to find. In interviews with the president of Ombudsman, he indicated that his firm has continued to grow and expand and that the market would support entry of new firms at this time.
24. Richard Hatley and James Ritter, "Prediction of Voting Behavior in Local School District Financial Referenda," paper presented at the Annual Meeting of the American Educational Research Association, Los Angeles, California, April 13–17, 1981, ED 203 509.
25. Oliver Williamson, "The Modern Corporation: Origins, Evolution, Attributes," *Journal of Economic Literature* 19 (December 1981), pp. 1537–1568.

HENRY M. LEVIN

Costs and Cost-Effectiveness of Computer-Assisted Instruction

Computer-assisted instruction (CAI) has been used in American elementary and secondary schools for two decades. Early applications of computers to education were based upon the use of a central mainframe computer linked to many schools over a large geographic area through telephone lines or minicomputers in which a central processing unit was connected to student terminals in a school or school district.[1] However, the recent interest in CAI has stemmed mainly from the introduction of microcomputers into the schools.

Microcomputers allow a higher degree of flexibility in deployment and use and do not require the elaborate communications networks associated with mainframe and minicomputers. A school can obtain a single microcomputer or multiple microcomputers. They can be placed in individual classrooms, a resource center, or computer laboratories, and they can be used as individual stations with highly diverse applications or for common instructional tasks. Although they can be linked to each other in local area networks, they can be used independently with no interconnections whatsoever.

Since about 1978 the compelling case for microcomputers in instruction stems not only from their flexibility, but from reductions in cost and increases in performance. Between 1978 and 1984, the cost for a given level of performance declined by 50 percent or more. This decline in cost, accompanied by the emerging centrality of computers in the workplace, has accelerated the purchase of microcomputers by schools and the integration of CAI into the school curriculum. By January of 1983 some 53 percent of all American schools and 85 percent of high schools had at least one computer, according to a major national survey, and the penetration of the microcomputer is certainly considerably higher today.[2]

The purpose of this study is to look more closely at the issue of cost and cost-effectiveness of the use of microcomputers for CAI. There are four popular assumptions on this subject which serve as a useful point of departure. These assumptions are: (1) that computer hardware accounts for most of the cost of delivering CAI; (2) that drastic declines in future costs of computers will create similar cost reductions for CAI; (3) that

Henry M. Levin is professor of education and economics and is affiliated with the Institute for Research on Educational Finance and Governance, Stanford University.

networks of microcomputers used for CAI are less costly than minicomputers with the same capabilities; and (4) that CAI has been found to be more cost-effective than other instructional alternatives.

Each of these assumptions will be evaluated according to the evidence that is available. But, before such an assessment can be undertaken, it is important to define costs, present a method of measuring costs, evaluate specifically the cost components of CAI, and provide some cost estimates for CAI services. The next section addresses the costs of CAI.

ESTIMATING THE COSTS OF CAI

What is the cost of CAI? When educators, policy makers, computer firms, and parents address the costs of CAI, they typically refer only to the costs of purchasing the microcomputers alone. Since a microcomputer with instructional capabilities costs less than $1000 and can last for several years, a school with 1000 students could acquire one microcomputer for every 20 students or 50 microcomputers for about $50,000. This would amount to the annual salaries of two teachers. But, since the computers would last for several years, the cost in a single year would be only a fraction of this. For example, if the machines were used for three years, the apparent cost would be only about $17,000 a year or $17 per student per year. Clearly such a cost seems very modest in comparison with the $3,000 or so spent annually on each student for all school services.

The problem with this type of calculation is that microcomputers in themselves are only one element in a more complex system for delivering instruction. In addition to the computers, schools need a secure facility to house them, curriculum software, knowledgeable personnel, provisions for maintenance, and other support services. The proper way to determine the cost of CAI is to ascertain what ingredients are needed to deliver a particular type and level of instructional services, to ascertain the cost of those ingredients, and to determine who pays for them. This approach is known as the resource or ingredients approach and represents a systematic and economically sound method for ascertaining costs.[3] In this context, we will use the words *ingredients* and *resources* interchangeably.

Before exploring the ingredients method and its application to CAI, it is useful to define what is meant by cost.[4] Cost refers to the value of what is given up by using resources in one way rather than in their best alternative use. The use of resources for one endeavor means that some other use of those resources is sacrificed or lost. The ingredients method is based upon this definition by evaluating in monetary terms the total value of all resources used in the CAI intervention. It is a comprehensive approach to determining all of the ingredients required for the intervention, assessing and summarizing their costs, and apportioning those costs among different constituencies, such as levels of government, parents, volunteers, and so on.

Identifying Ingredients

The first step in using the ingredients approach is to identify those that will be needed for a CAI intervention. These can generally be divided among personnel, facilities, equipment, materials and supplies, and all other. The personnel category includes virtually all of the human resources required including teaching specialists, coordinators, and administrators. Each position should be identified in terms of the proportion of a full-time position required as well as the qualifications of the person occupying the position. Facilities refers to the physical space required for the intervention. This may be a classroom or a portion of a classroom. The facility should be identified according to both the amount of space needed and its quality. For example, if security devices and air conditioning are required, these should be stipulated.

Equipment includes all of the hardware that will be required. In the case of a microcomputer intervention this will include the microcomputers, printers, and other devices required for the intervention. It may include such auxiliary equipment as cooling fans, antisurge devices, and added peripheral equipment such as disk drives or cassette recorders. Materials and supplies include the curriculum software, instructional manuals, paper for the printers, and other requirements.

The "all other" or miscellaneous category should include the costs of energy (heating, lighting, and power), routine maintenance of classrooms, hardware maintenance, fire and theft insurance, and training. The hardware maintenance and insurance could alternatively be included in the equipment category rather than the miscellaneous one. If specific administrative positions cannot be identified for the personnel category, it may be useful to make some estimate of administrative overhead in this category to cover the purchasing, contracting, and other arrangements that will have to be made by the principal and the central office staff of the school district.

The guiding principle for listing the ingredients of the proposed CAI project is to be as complete as possible, especially for the major inputs. It is important to remember that one copy of software is not adequate for multiple microcomputers. In general, a copy must be purchased for all students who will use the software simultaneously or an agreement must be negotiated with the software manufacturer that permits the school to pay a fee to produce a specified number of copies for internal use. Although it may be tempting to buy a single copy and duplicate it, such an activity is illegal.

Valuing Ingredients

Once the ingredients that are required for the CAI intervention are stipulated, it is necessary to determine their cost. There is a standard methodology for doing this that is readily available, and space precludes replicating these details.[5] However, it is useful to indicate some of the principles for setting out the costs of ingredients. First, all ingredients are costed, even if they appear to be "free." The reason for this is that even contributed inputs such as the time of a volunteer or a donation are not free to the donor, even though they do not have a cost to the school or school district. In those cases, we wish to acknowledge the costs, even though at a later stage we will apportion them to other constituencies than the school and school district. This is not only desirable for purposes of completeness, but it is also important to recognize such costs in the event that donations of volunteer time and other resources are not obtainable so that they may make a claim on school resources at some future time.

Second, costs are set out at their market values for the same reason. Take the case of a classroom that is provided for a computer laboratory. At a budgetary level there appears to be no cost because there is no financial transaction. However, given the concept of "opportunity cost" for ingredients, there is always a cost as long as the resource has alternative uses. In the case of a classroom, that space could be used for other instructional purposes or for administrative functions, or it could be leased to outside users for day care, senior citizen, or commercial uses. In an age of declining enrollments many school districts have sold buildings or leased portions of school facilities that were unused. By using such "extra" space for CAI, the school district sacrifices what it could have obtained by leasing the facility. Accordingly, there is a cost to using a classroom for CAI as opposed to using it for other purposes, even though these costs will not be found on accounting statements.

Third, as suggested by these first two principles, budget or accounting statements do not include all of the costs of an intervention. Not only do they exclude resources for which there is no budgetary transaction such as the donated ones or employment of available space that has other competing uses, but they provide a misleading view of annual costs for any equipment purchases. The reason for this is that equipment such as a microcomputer has an expected life of three to six years, depending upon its use and maintenance. However, conventional school accounting practices require that the entire amount be budgeted during the year of purchase so that the annual estimated costs in the first year are overestimated by including the complete cost of equipment in that year. In subsequent years the cost of CAI is underestimated because the cost of equipment is not reflected in the budget. Yet, consider that the costs should be spread over all of the years of use to get an accurate picture of the annual cost of CAI. Although this practice of apportioning costs over the lifetime of equipment is a standard one in cost accounting, it is not common in the construction of school budgets. Thus, one should not rely completely on school budgets if one wishes to obtain an accurate picture of annual costs of an intervention.

Finally, it is useful to state costs in annual terms. They can then be readily compared with the annual costs of other possible interventions as well as the overall annual costs of school operations. Accordingly, all of the analyses that follow will be based upon the estimate of annual costs, although the initial costs of acquiring microcomputers that will last a number of years will be noted.

Given this background, it is possible to suggest some principles for estimating the costs of each category. Costs are generally easiest to estimate for the personnel category. The reason for this is that any school district can ascertain readily what it needs to pay for most types of instructional personnel. These costs should include not only salaries, but fringe benefits as well. In the case of volunteers, the estimate should be based upon what it would cost the school or school district if paid staff had to be hired for such positions.

Facilities costs can be estimated in a number of ways. The easiest is to ascertain the leased value of equivalent space. This can be done by specifying the amount of space and its characteristics and checking with a local real estate firm to determine what such space would cost in that location. A different method is to determine the replacement cost of the facility and to convert the replacement cost into an annual value based upon the lifetime of the facility and the interest rate that reflects the "opportunity cost" of using resources for capital investment.

The annual cost of equipment can be estimated in a similar manner. If one knows the purchase price and life of the equipment and the pertinent interest rate, one can use a simple table of "annualization factors" to determine the annual cost.[6] Clearly, the greater the lifetime of the equipment, the lower the annual cost. In some cases it is desirable to include the insurance costs for fire and theft as well as maintenance costs of the equipment in the equipment category rather than in the miscellaneous one. Both of these are easily ascertainable because they are generally paid for on an annual basis, often as a percentage of the value of the equipment.

The most important component of the materials and supplies category is likely to be the curriculum software. If it is leased for an annual fee, its annual cost is easily ascertained. If it is purchased, its annual cost can be derived in a similar fashion to that of the hardware, although it should be remembered that the software may have a different lifetime than the hardware. The annual cost of other materials and supplies can be estimated on the basis of the costs of the ingredients that are needed for this category.

Finally, the miscellaneous or other ingredients can be valued according to their particular characteristics. The costs of energy use and facilities maintenance can generally be estimated on the basis of school experience for these categories. Training will include not only the direct cost of instructors and materials, but also the reimbursement of salaries of trainees during the training sessions. To the degree that the trainees are expected to stay for a number of years without requiring annual retraining, the initial costs of training can be "annualized" in a way similar to that of the equipment and the software.

In summary, a standard set of procedures can be used to estimate the costs of the ingredients required for CAI. Once these costs are estimated, they can be added to obtain the total costs for the intervention on an annual basis. They can also be divided into those that will be borne by the school or school district and by others, and they can be used to estimate the initial "out-of-pocket" costs that the school district will need to initiate the intervention.

Apportioning Costs

The ingredients method requires that all resources required for the intervention be stipulated and their costs be ascertained. This approach provides a complete picture of resource needs and their costs and can be used to determine the overall cost of the intervention. However, a school or school district will be concerned primarily with its share of the total costs. It is in the interest of the district to obtain as much outside assistance as possible in order to reduce its own costs. For example, it may be possible to get community volunteers to undertake some of the personnel responsibilities, particularly those of aides who will assist students in using the microcomputers. It is also common for computer firms to provide at least some equipment to schools at no cost. The state of California has enacted legislation that provides tax credits to computer manufacturers for making such donations. Even in the absence of such legislation firms have incentives to give equipment to schools in order to get tax deductions and to prime both the schools and home (parental) market for their products. Finally, some of the states provide subsidies to schools to promote computer instruction, and federal grants can be used to pay for all or some of the cost of CAI under the Education Consolidation and Improvement Act (ECIA).

After determining the full cost of the intervention when the value of all resources is accounted for, it is useful to divide the costs among those who bear them. In this way, it is possible to distinguish among costs that will be borne by the school district, other government agencies, volunteers, and private firms or other donors. This analysis also permits a determination of the types of support that the program will depend upon and the areas in which the school district will have to increase its share if the subsidies and donations do not materialize.

Initial Costs

A separate analysis can also be made of the initial or "up-front" costs. Such costs refer to those expenditures that must be made at the outset of the intervention, even though the acquisitions and improvements will last for several years and will not require additional outlay. The best examples are the refurbishing of classrooms into computer laboratories and the acquisition of computers and software. In these cases the usual practice is to pay for the improvements and equipment at the outset, even though good business practice would normally lead to financing them over their lifetimes. However, in the case of schools, only major capital construction is financed through borrowing. Refurbishing of buildings and acquisition of equipment are paid for immediately upon their completion or purchase. The ingredients method facilitates a separate accounting of any resources that must be paid for initially in order to calculate up-front costs. Of course, the leasing of computers and software as well as facilities, such as temporary classrooms, represents a way of reducing the initially high costs of financing this type of intervention.

Summary of Cost Analysis

This section has provided a brief summary of a method for ascertaining the costs of CAI. The main principles of the approach are the identification and stipulation of all ingredients—not just computer hardware; the costing of all ingredients according to their market value; the apportionment of costs among the various constituencies who will be expected to bear them; and the determination of what initial or up-front investment will be required by the school or school district to undertake the CAI program. In the next section these principles will be applied to ascertaining the costs of CAI in order to evaluate four popular assumptions on the subject.

ACTUAL COSTS OF CAI

The principles that were set out above have been used to estimate a major application of CAI in 1978 and in 1984.[7] However, before presenting these results, it is important to emphasize that they should be viewed as illustrative rather than definitive. The reason for this is that there are many different approaches to CAI, and there are many different settings. Each application may have different ingredient requirements and service levels as well as goals. In addition, costs for particular ingredients such as personnel may differ substantially among different settings. The advantage of the following examples is that they have been derived from one of the most widespread uses of CAI. In addition, they permit an examination of changes in cost levels and structure over time, as well as a comparison of the costs of microcomputers and minicomputers for producing the same type and level of services.

The specific application of CAI that we will consider is that of "drill-and-practice." Drill-and-practice refers to the use of computer exercises to reinforce classroom instruction. It is the earliest application of computers to learning and has been used for at least two decades.[8] A 1983 survey of schools found it to be the second most important computer application, occupying 23 percent of all student instructional time on computers at the elementary and secondary levels.[9] Rigorous evaluations of computer drill-and-practice suggest that the intervention has strong positive effects on student achievement in mathematics and reading.[10]

The most widely used and evaluated drill-and-practice approach is that of the Computer Curriculum Corporation (CCC). A prominent four-year evaluation of the CCC application was carried out in Los Angeles from 1976–1980, sponsored by the National Institute of Education and carried out by the Educational Testing Service.[11] In that intervention, elementary students were provided with ten-minute daily sessions of drill-and-practice in mathematics, reading, and language arts. Some students had more than one daily session, and the combination of subjects to which students were assigned differed so that a child studying reading and language arts by computer could serve as a control for assessing the benefits of mathematics instruction for another child studying reading, language arts, and mathematics. Since the experiment ran for four years, it was also possible to make comparisons among students with up to four years of CAI and with different combinations of subjects as well as between students who had received CAI and those who had not.

The approach evaluated in the study requires a separate classroom with 32 terminals connected to a minicomputer. (A similar type of delivery system can be constructed using microcomputers that are arranged in a local network with a hard-disk storage device.) The minicomputer holds all computer curricula for all elementary grades and curriculum areas as well as student records on the number of sessions that students have taken and their progress. Since each terminal was used for about 23 sessions a day, the computer facility was able to accommodate a total of 736 sessions a day.

Personnel include a full-time coordinator and two part-time teaching aides as well as a small portion of administrative time. The CAI coordinator is responsible for the over-

TABLE 1

Computer-Assisted Instruction Ingredients and Costs, Minicomputer System. Number of Students: 736 (includes 23 sessions per terminal per day for 32 terminals).

ANNUAL COST	INGREDIENT
	Personnel
$25,000	1 CAI coordinator at $20,000 plus fringe benefits per year
6,000	2 teaching aides at 600 hours at $5.00/hour
1,750	1 principal at 5% time at $28,000 plus fringe benefits
	Facilities
5,775	Classroom for CAI laboratory (includes $1,000 for utilities and routine maintenance of the space)
3,010	Classroom renovation for CAI laboratory
244	Furnishings (includes teacher desk and chair and student chairs only)
	Equipment and Materials
4,982*	1 Microhost (CPU) with 1 Mb memory and 40 Mb storage at $21,700, annualized at 10% interest over 6 years
4,857*	32 Computer Curriculum Corporation terminals at $21,152, annualized at 10% interest over 6 years
207*	1 dot matrix (120 cps) printer at $900, annualized at 10% interest over 6 years
11,434*	Software at $49,800, annualized at 10% interest over 6 years
1,102*	Installation at $4,800, annualized at 10% interest over 6 years (includes CPT at $1,500, terminals at $3,200, and printer at $100)
6,400	Curriculum rental per year
3,000	Supplies
	Other
40	Training time for coordinator at 1½ days × $100/day, annualized at 10% interest over 5 years
855	Training time for 40 teachers at 4 hours × $20.25/hour, annualized at 10% interest over 5 years
9,720	Maintenance (includes CPU at $3,600, terminals at $5,760, and printer at $360)
3,000	Insurance
87,376	**Total cost per year**
119	**Cost per student**

*Costs quoted by Computer Curriculum Corporation as of March 16, 1984.

---

all functioning of the CAI program including scheduling and coordination of instruction, reporting to teachers on student progress, and monitoring equipment functioning and maintenance. This role is served by a classroom teacher who is trained in an intensive one and one-half day program. Teaching aides monitor the performance of students and assist them in understanding the CAI problems and solving them. In addition to the computer hardware and personnel, other inputs include a renovated classroom, curriculum rental, supplies, insurance, and maintenance.

Table 1 provides a summary of the ingredients and costs of the CAI system for a 32-terminal laboratory. Details for the cost analysis are found in Levin, Glass, and Meister (1984). The overall cost is about $87,000 per year or about $119 per year for a ten-minute daily session. Hardware and software costs are based upon data for the spring of 1984, while all other cost data are for 1980. Thus, overall costs would be somewhat higher in 1984 for the latter category. What is most instructive is the breakdown in costs among categories. The annualized cost of hardware (cost per year) accounts for only about 11 percent of the total cost, while personnel costs account for about 38 percent. Curriculum and other software costs represent 21 percent of the total, and hardware maintenance about 11 percent.

How Dominant is the Cost of the Computer?

This cost breakdown enables us to address the first popular assumption, namely that the cost of computer hardware dominates the cost of CAI. In this example, the cost of computer hardware represented only about one-ninth of the overall annual cost of providing CAI services. It is also important to note that although personnel accounted for about two-fifths of costs, or over three times that of the computer hardware, staffing was relatively modest for such a busy facility with over 700 student sessions a day. The only personnel were a full-time coordinator ($20,000 per year plus fringe benefits), two part-time teaching aides (600 hours each at $5.00 per hour for a total of $6,000 a year), and a small amount of administrator time. It is reasonable to believe that this is probably a minimal staffing pattern for a facility with 32 terminals that are fully utilized for the entire school day. It should be noted that several years of experience suggest that full utilization meant about 23 ten-minute sessions a day or the equivalent of four hours of continuous use over a six-hour school day. The remaining time was accounted for by that required for maintenance and testing of equipment, production of student records, lost time because of inoperative equipment, and time required during the transition from one student group to another.

Nor can one argue that this cost pattern is unique to a minicomputer with terminals in contrast to microcomputers. A similar microcomputer configuration is likely to be faced with similar staffing needs. Further, maintenance and software needs are not likely to be substantially different between minicomputers and microcomputers with the same service capacity. Indeed, in a later comparison of the costs of mini- and microcomputers, it will be suggested that as of 1984 costs are roughly comparable or even favor the minicomputer over microcomputer networks with communication capabilities.

In large measure an understanding of all costs of CAI explains why school districts are unable to utilize efficiently the microcomputers that they purchase without making explicit logistical and cost provisions for other requirements. The purchase of microcomputers is a necessary condition—but not a sufficient one—for providing CAI services. For every dollar spent on such hardware some four or more dollars of other resources will be needed such as supporting software, maintenance, personnel, and special facilities. The overall message is that although computer hardware may be the most visible component of a CAI delivery system, it accounts for a relatively small portion of the total costs of CAI. This is a lesson that is important for schools to learn if they are to provide CAI services rather than to limit themselves to the purchase of computers with the hope that the services will be produced automatically from the hardware.

Will the Costs of CAI Fall Drastically?

A second popular assumption is that the costs of providing CAI services will decline drastically with concomitant declines in the costs of computers. This proposition can be examined both historically and logically. As part of the evaluation of the Los Angeles experiment, a cost analysis was undertaken in 1978.[12] The overall cost of delivering 736 daily CAI sessions per year was estimated to be about $100,000 for the 1977–78 school year. The cost per year for a daily CAI session was estimated at $136 per student. Recall that the estimated cost of providing the same services in 1984 was about $119 per year for each student for a daily CAI session. Accordingly, even with substantial declines in the cost of the computer hardware between 1978 and 1984, the cost of providing CAI instruction had declined by only about 12.5 percent.

Let us examine this paradox more carefully. In 1978 the annual cost of computer hardware was estimated to be about 28 percent of the total annual cost of providing the CAI. What would happen to such costs if the hardware costs had declined by 50 percent? The answer is that there would have been a 14 percent reduction in the overall costs of service delivery, or half of 28 percent. According to the 1984 estimates, the actual share of hardware costs had declined to only 11 percent of total costs. This reduction in the proportion of cost attributable to hardware was due not only to a decline in hardware costs per se, but also to relative rises in the costs of some of the other ingredients.

A bold hypothetical exercise might assume that hardware costs decline so drastically in future years that computers will be given away at no cost whatsoever. Although this is an absurd assumption, it is useful for seeing the limit to which a reduction in hardware costs can diminish the overall costs of CAI. Clearly, the use of free computers would reduce the cost of CAI services by only 11 percent in this example, as long as need for the other ingredients and their costs remained constant. Of course, to the degree that the cost of other ingredients, such as personnel, increase over time, not all of the cost reduction from free computers will be reflected in reduced costs of CAI services. In that case the cost decline would be less than 11 percent.

The popular assumption that the costs of CAI will decline drastically with reductions in hardware costs is inconsistent with basic arithmetic. It is only if improvements in hardware reduce the need or the cost of other ingredients that such an outcome would take place. Yet it is difficult to see how a high level of computer utilization could be integrated into school curricula without at least minimal coordination and staffing, investment in software, adequate facilities, and so on. Neither the recent history nor the structure of CAI costs supports the view that there will be drastic declines in the costs of CAI services. It is only when CAI services are defined as the mere availability of computers that the view makes sense. As noted above, however, such a definition is naive and educationally indefensible.

Are Microcomputers Cheaper than Minicomputers?

The remarkable upsurge in popularity of microcomputers and their amazing flexibility and performance have contributed to the popular assumption that CAI is synony-

COST-EFFECTIVENESS OF CAI

A fourth popular belief is the view that the decline in cost of computers and rise in their capabilities as well as the explosion in availability of educational software have made CAI a more cost-effective alternative to instruction than traditional approaches. While this may be the case, rarely is evidence used to back up the claim. Cost-effectiveness studies require that systematic analyses of costs be available for addressing the same educational outcomes.[16] The relative lack of data on both costs and effects suggests that a high priority be attached to rigorous studies of the cost-effectiveness of CAI.

Recent research undertaken at the Institute for Research on Educational Finance and Governance (IFG) attempted to compare the cost-effectiveness of drill-and-practice CAI with that of three other alternatives for increasing student achievement in mathematics and reading in elementary schools.[17] The other interventions that were considered in the analysis were reducing class size, increasing instructional time, and cross-age tutoring. Both CAI and increasing instructional time have been featured prominently among the recommendations of the national reports on educational reform, while reducing class size and cross-age tutoring represent more traditional approaches. The emphasis in selecting specific forms of the interventions was to choose those that were replicable in elementary schools (as opposed to those developed for experimental purposes), that had reasonable evaluation data from which to estimate effectiveness, and that had sufficient detail to facilitate identification of ingredients and their costs.

The specific CAI intervention that was evaluated is based upon the CCC drill-and-practice curriculum described previously. The intervention for increasing instructional time entailed the addition of one hour of instruction per day, half of it devoted to mathematics and half devoted to reading. The main ingredient for costing purposes was additional teacher time. Cross-age tutoring refers to a peer component, the tutoring of younger students by older ones under the supervision of adults for grades 2 and 3, and an adult component comprised of adult tutoring of students in grades 5 and 6. The specific tutoring program chosen for this study was the Cross-Age Structured Tutoring Program for Reading and Mathematics in the Boise (Idaho) Schools. Staffing for each elementary school of about 300 to 400 students includes a tutor manager in reading, a tutor manager in mathematics, and an adult tutor for each subject. Daily tutoring sessions last about 20 minutes a day using a commercially available curriculum. The reduction of class size was based upon examining the costs and effects of reducing class size incrementally from 35 to 30 students; 30 to 25 students; 25 to 20 students; and 35 to 20 students. Costs of this intervention are associated with the additional classrooms and teachers that are required.

Effectiveness

The effectiveness of each of the interventions was estimated by doing a two stage analysis, details of which can be found in Glass.[18] First, the available evaluations for

TABLE 2
Estimated Effectiveness of Four Educational Interventions
in Months of Additional Student Gain
per Year of Instruction

		Mathematics	**Reading**
CAI		1.2	2.3
Cross-age tutoring:			
Peer component		9.7	4.8
Adult component		6.7	3.8
Increasing instructional time		0.3	0.7
Reducing class size:			
From	*To*		
35	30	0.6	0.3
30	25	0.7	0.4
25	20	0.9	0.5
35	20	2.2	1.1

each class of intervention were assessed to obtain a range of their effects on student achievement. Second, evaluations of the specific interventions for CAI, increasing instructional time, and cross-age tutoring were assessed to obtain specific estimates of achievement effects. The effects of reductions in class size were derived from a meta-analysis of about 80 evaluations on the subject. The results of the first and second stage were compared to assure that the specific interventions were representative of those of the classes of interventions chosen.

Table 2 shows the estimated effectiveness of each of the interventions. Since the interventions represent supplements to existing instruction, the effects are evaluated in terms of the additional achievement expected for children receiving each intervention relative to similar students who are not exposed to it. Effect sizes were estimated in terms of achievement gains in standard deviation units. However, a standard deviation at the elementary level is approximately equal to a year of achievement, where an academic year is equal to ten months. Accordingly, achievement results have been converted into months of student gain per year of instruction to provide a more familiar measure of achievement. Table 2 shows the expected monthly gains in achievement of students for each intervention, where each month of gain is about one-tenth of a school year of achievement.

The CAI intervention produced a healthy result with over a month of student gain in, mathematics and over two months, almost a quarter of a year, in reading for a ten-minute daily session in each subject over the school year. However, even larger effects were found for both the peer and adult components of cross-age tutoring. Peer tutoring

TABLE 3
Cost per Student per Subject of Four Educational Interventions

		Cost per Student per Subject
CAI		$119
Cross-age tutoring:		
Peer component		212
Adult component		827
Increasing instructional time		61
Reducing class size:		
From	*To*	
35	30	45
30	25	63
25	20	94
35	20	201

produced gains of almost a full year in mathematics achievement and half a year in reading achievement, and gains from adult tutoring were almost as impressive. In contrast, reductions in class size showed less than a month of gain in both mathematics and reading for each five-student decrement. The direct reduction from 35 to 20 students, however, was associated with gains similar to CAI, but with greater achievement gains in mathematics than reading. Finally, the effectiveness of an additional half hour of instruction in each subject showed very small gains.

Table 3 shows the costs per student of each intervention. The cost per student per subject represents the total value of resources required to replicate each intervention divided by the number of students receiving the instructional benefits, where the ingredients method was used to estimate costs. The most costly of the interventions was adult tutoring, followed by peer tutoring and a reduction in class size from 35 to 20. The cost of CAI was about half that of peer tutoring. Reductions in class size by five-student decrements and increasing instructional time by one half hour a day in each subject were the least costly interventions.

When costs for each intervention in Table 3 are combined with the effectiveness results from Table 2, cost-effectiveness ratios are obtained. With these it is possible to ascertain the expected gains in student achievement associated with a given cost. Table 4 shows the gains in student achievement from each intervention for each $100 cost per pupil. The CAI intervention is estimated to produce a gain of about one month in mathematics and two months in reading for each $100 in cost per student. In contrast, peer tutoring is associated with almost half a year of achievement gain in mathematics and almost a quarter year in reading. Other interventions tend to show lower cost-effectiveness than either peer tutoring or CAI. Indeed, even though adult tutoring showed one of the highest effects, its high cost creates a cost-effectiveness ratio that is among the lowest of the four interventions.

Based upon these results, it appears that the specific CAI intervention evaluated in

TABLE 4
**Estimated Effectiveness of Four Educational Interventions
in Months of Additional Student Achievement Gain per Year
of Instruction for Each $100 Cost per Student**

			Mathematics	Reading
CAI			1.0	1.9
Cross-age tutoring:				
Peer component			4.6	2.2
Adult component			0.8	0.5
Increasing instructional time			0.5	1.2
Reducing class size:				
	From	*To*		
	35	30	1.4	0.7
	30	25	1.2	0.6
	25	20	1.0	0.5
	35	20	1.1	0.6

this study was more cost-effective than adult tutoring, reducing class size, or increasing instructional time. However, it was considerably less cost-effective than peer tutoring in mathematics and slightly less cost-effective in reading. This suggests that the CAI intervention does perform comparatively well according to cost-effectiveness criteria, although it is not necessarily the most cost-effective approach to improving mathematics and reading achievement in the elementary grades. Although these results are based upon CAI delivery with minicomputers rather than microcomputers, analysis of microcomputers for this specific CAI intervention suggests that they would be more costly and would be associated with lower rather than higher cost-effectiveness ratios.[19]

Of course, as new developments occur in CAI curricula and their applications, CAI might improve its relative cost-effectiveness. Evidence at the present time suggests, however, that educators should not assume blindly that CAI is a more cost-effective intrevention than other alternatives. Clearly, the overall choice must depend upon a school's instructional goals, available resources for reaching those goals, proficiency in using computers, and many other factors.

The overriding theme of this paper is that popular assumptions about costs and cost-effectiveness of CAI are often not supported by evidence. To the degree that decisions to adopt CAI are made on the basis of such assumptions, they may be costly and inefficient. It is crucial that systematic evaluation of CAI proceed as rapidly as the proliferation of computers in instruction in order to ascertain the most promising applications in a framework which considers both their educational effectiveness and their costs.

NOTES

This paper will also appear in the 1986 Yearbook of the National Society for the Study of Education (NSSE) on ''Education and Micro-electronic Technologies,'' edited by Jack Culbertson and Vern Cunningham. The research was supported by funding from the National Institute of Education to the Institute for Research on Educational Finance and Governance under the project on "Costs and Cost-Effectiveness of Educational Interventions."

1. D. Alpert and D.L. Bitzer, "Advances in Computer-Based Education," *Science* 166 (March 1970); and Patrick Suppes and Mona Morningstar, "Computer-Assisted Instruction," *Science* 166 (1969), pp. 343–350.
2. Center for Social Organizations of Schools, *School Uses of Microcomputers* 2 (Baltimore: Johns Hopkins University, 1983).
3. Henry M. Levin, *Cost-Effectiveness: A Primer* (Beverly Hills, CA: Sage Publications, 1983).
4. Ibid., chapter 3.
5. Ibid., chapter 4.
6. Ibid., pp. 67–71.
7. Henry M. Levin and Louis Woo, "An Evaluation of Costs of Computer-Assisted Instruction," *Economics of Education Review* 1 (Winter), pp. 1–26; and Henry M. Levin, Gene Glass, and Gail Meister, "A Cost-Effectiveness Analysis of Four Educational Interventions," IFG Project Report No. 84-A11 (Stanford, CA: Institute for Research on Educational Finance and Governance, 1984).
8. Suppes and Morningstar.
9. Center for Social Organizations of Schools, *School Uses of Microcomputers* 1 (Baltimore: Johns Hopkins University, 1983), p. 7.
10. Gene V. Glass, "The Effectiveness of Four Educational Interventions," IFG Project Report No. 84-A19 (Stanford, CA: Institute for Research on Educational Finance and Governance, 1984); and Marjorie Ragosta, Paul W. Holland, and Dean T. Jamison, *Computer-Assisted Instruction and Compensatory Education: The ETS/LAUSD Study*, Final Report, Project Report No. 19 (Princeton, NJ: Educational Testing Service, 1982).
11. Ragosta, Holland, and Jamison.
12. Levin and Woo.
13. Philip K. Piele, "Local Area Networks for Microcomputers in Education," (paper presented at the Third Annual Conference on the Computer: Extension of the Human Mind, Center for Advanced Technology in Education, University of Oregon, 1984).
14. Gail R. Meister, "Successful Integration of Microcomputers in an Elementary School," IFG Project Report No. 84-A13 (Stanford, CA: Institute for Research on Educational Finance and Governance, 1984).
15. Levin, Glass, and Meister, pp. 23–25.
16. Levin.
17. Levin, Glass, and Meister.
18. Glass.
19. Levin, Glass, and Meister, pp. 23–25 and appendix tables A-6.1 and A-6.2.

RICHARD R. VALENCIA

Public School Closures and Policy Issues: Financial and Social Implications

Two decades ago education in the United States was being hailed as the new growth industry. In the late 1960s and early 1970s, however, declining enrollments caught the schools by surprise.[1] A decline in the birthrate and an aging population meant fewer students enrolled in public schools. Adverse economic conditions such as rising inflation and a mounting societal dissatisfaction with levels of student achievement in the schools resulted in an erosion of public support and a diminished willingness to invest in education, particularly in a period of decline.[2] At the same time, competition between educational interest groups such as bilingual education and special education garnered the support of some politicians in passing legislation, resulting in "mandates without money."[3] The resulting factionalism created enormous pressures for school districts throughout the country to deal head on with the problems and conflicts of managing school systems with declining enrollments. School administrators and school boards implemented numerous types of fiscal belt-tightening strategies to accommodate the decline in resources brought about by shrinking enrollments and exacerbated by growing inflation. One particular cost-saving measure that school districts used with some frequency, because it was believed to make common and fiscal sense to do so, was the closure of underutilized schools. It has been estimated that in the 1970s over 7,000 schools, affecting about 80 percent of the nation's school districts, were closed.[4]

In the last one and a half decades a voluminous and expanding literature on school closures has developed.[5] The bulk of these studies, however, is largely prescriptive.[6] That is, these investigations deal primarily with the advice and technical aspects of retrenchment—how to consolidate programs, how to decide the criteria for closures. Very few studies are concerned with the policy implications of closures on students and the community. The purpose of this paper is to examine the implications of school closures according to four criteria: (a) School closures increase enrollments in the remaining schools. Is bigger necessarily better? (b) School closures are purported to be cost-beneficial. Do closures actually result in substantial cost savings? (c) School closures—by their very nature—are burdensome and raise issues of equity. Are closures in multi-ethnic communities "color blind"? Are closures in socioeconomically

Richard R. Valencia is assistant professor of education and psychology at the University of California at Santa Cruz.

diverse communities equitable? (d) School closures are contentious technical and political processes. Do closures tend to erode public support for education?

Before the analysis gets underway, two caveats are in order. First, the issues are exceedingly complex. A major thesis of this paper is that school closures—in terms of causes and effects—are not simple phenomena. Thus, no simple, unequivocal answers should be expected. Second, the state-of-the-art on school closures with respect to policy implications and the overall impact on communities is in a nascent stage. As one researcher observes:

> Until the literature on declining enrollment and consolidation breaks away from either cookbooks giving recipes to administrators on how to avoid the lash of community anger or research on the technology of projections, little more about political impact will be uncovered.[7]

In light of this, the present analysis will rely on some occasional hypothesizing and intellectual risk-taking.

SCHOOL SIZE ISSUE

One immediate outcome of school closures is that students go from schools of lower enrollment to consolidated schools of higher enrollment. The resultant consolidation means the receiving schools increase in size. Therefore, it is clear that the issues of size and its relation to education expenditures and student outcomes, such as achievement, have significant bearing on policy decisions in an era of retrenchment. In closure decisions, a major hypothesis operative in the minds of school board members and other policy makers is that larger schools are in a better position to offer a broader curriculum with more courses at lower costs compared to smaller schools. Often, this conjecture has led to the conclusion that a major solution to the problem of rising costs is to increase school size.[8] On what basis is the perceived relation between larger schools and increased school effectiveness made? Lindsay's answer to this is revealing:

> The paths followed by educational policy during the last half century with respect to school size have been guided more by intuition than science. The dominant assumption has been that the larger the school, the more economical, specialized, comprehensive, and effective it must be. In short, bigger is better.[9]

When one looks to the available literature on the relation between school size and student outcome, however, intuition takes a back seat. In a classic study two decades ago, Barker and Gump examined the relations among school size, school setting (extracurricular and classroom), and student participation and satisfaction in 13 Kansas high schools ranging in size from 18 to 2,287 students.[10] The major finding, which supported previous research, was a negative relation between institutional size and quantity and quality of student participation. In a recent study, Lindsay replicated several of Barker and Gump's findings with a representative sample of students at the national level.[11] The study is significant because the observed relation between school size and student participation still held when socioeconomic status and academic ability were controlled. Although the empirical evidence is by no means conclusive, there are numerous other studies indicating the cognitive and affective advantage of smaller over larger schools and demystifying the alleged superiority of larger schools.[12]

If the evidence leans toward the conclusion that small schools are better than large ones, is there an optimal size? There are no hard findings on this issue. There are some opinions, however, by scholars who have worked in this area. Levin proposes that there is no educational argument for elementary schools being larger than 300–350 students and for secondary schools containing more than 300–400 students. "As a rule of thumb," Levin notes, [schools are probably too big] "if the principal and teachers do not know most of the students."[13] In one of the most comprehensive studies of schooling in the United States, Goodlad argues there are no defensible reasons for operating elementary schools with more than 300 students or secondary schools with more than 500–600 students.[14] Contending that we need further, sustained research on the school size issue, Goodlad posits: "The burden of proof . . . is on large size."[15] On the question of optimal size, Barker and Gump's advice is:

> The educational process is a subtle and delicate one about which we know little, but it surely thrives on participation, enthusiasm, and responsibility. Our findings and our theory posit a negative relationship between school size and individual student participation. What seems to happen is that as schools get larger and settings inevitably become more heavily populated, more of the students are less needed; they become superfluous, redundant.

> What size should a school be? The data of this research and our own educational values tell us that a school should be sufficiently small that all of its students are needed for its enterprises. A school should be small enough that students are not redundant.[16]

The policy implication stemming from research on the school size issue appears clear. Since size is a fairly manipulative variable, "educational policymakers do have some control over the size of schools, especially in a time of declining enrollment."[17]

COST SAVINGS ISSUE

The ostensible driving force for most school closures is that of cost savings. This mind set has led educators and the public to focus on drastic measures to cut costs, particularly the closing of schools.[18] One reason that underutilized or near-empty schools have become the prime targets of cost-cutting strategies is that they are highly visible. After all, can one slight the public's reaction and right to question "why should half-empty schools remain open when schooling costs are soaring?" No, there is nothing wrong with raising the issue. What is questionable, however, is the assumption that closing schools will result in huge financial savings. On the contrary, the projected cost savings of closing schools are often exaggerated. School closures in most cases mean only slight savings because 75–85 percent of a school budget is for personnel costs, which are usually only affected slightly, if at all, by closures.[19] Furthermore, in many cases additional costs may rise—transportation of displaced students, maintenance, insurance, and security for closed buildings.

Is there empirical evidence on how much is saved by school closures? Not only is there meager data to support the closure-savings argument, but most districts that have closed schools simply are unable to document the amount of money saved.[20] For example, Seattle has closed a number of schools over a 10-year period. Yet, citizens charged that school administrators could still not report how much money was saved by the closure of a single school.[21] In an extensive study of school closures in 49 school districts throughout the country, Andrews collected survey data on both estimated and actual cost savings after closures of elementary schools.[22] Of the 49 districts, 35 had projected savings before closures. Of these, only 12 districts calculated the actual cost savings subsequent to the closings. Andrews reports that 4 of the 12 districts reported cost savings; the savings ranged from $2,000 to $60,000 and the estimated savings were less than initially projected. On the other hand, 50 percent of the districts calculated that no money had been saved. Finally, two districts reported that the closings had actually cost money. In short, 8 of the 12 districts concluded that the school closures resulted in no savings or additional costs.

It should be noted, however, that there are likely to be instances where cost savings resulting from closures are substantial. For example, it would appear that in some cases building maintenance and energy costs in underenrolled schools are so enormous, as in the Northeast, that consolidation would be in order. But closures such as these do not seem to be the rule.

In conclusion, although there is little solid data on the cost-benefit issue of school closures, one can infer from the literature that closing schools reduces per-pupil costs very little, if at all. Thus, it appears that the strategy of closing schools to save money is largely symbolic. As noted in one study, "The savings for the taxpayer is psychological only."[23] From a policy perspective, it appears appropriate to ask, "Why waste time, money, and community goodwill on a task that will not reap overriding financial rewards?"[24] Generally, closures may not be worth the added costs to parents of additional student time and parental costs in transportation to the receiving schools. Further, it might not be worth the loss in educational benefits resulting from small school size.

EQUITY ISSUE

A cold fact of life regarding retrenchment policy making is that conflict-management decisions tend to result in clear winners and losers. On this point, a major conclusion of school closure research by Boyd and Wheaton is:

> The politics of school closings is more a "divide and conquer" than a "plan and agree" process. The secret of school closings, sensed by some school officials, is *concentrated cuts judiciously targeted* to minimize the likelihood of the formation of resistant coalitions. There always will be opposition to school closings, but if it is isolated it will have little effect. Because citizens in other neighborhoods do not mind seeing someone else's ox get gored, they will be unlikely to join forces with the losers unless they believe their neighborhood schools will be in jeopardy.[25]

In urban, multi-ethnic, socioeconomically diverse segregated school districts, which characterize most of the nation's large urban centers, school closures raise critical issues of educational equity. Based on a small number of case studies, there is ample evidence that economically advantaged white students and their parents have been the clear winners, while minority and working-class students and their parents have been the clear losers as a result of closure decisions. Investigations of school closures in Nashville, New York, Phoenix, Santa Barbara, and St. Louis have reported that schools with primarily low socioeconomic status and minority students have suffered the brunt, if not the exclusive burden, of closings.[26] In these cities, poor minority schools have been disproportionately closed while more affluent white schools have been disproportionately left open. Forcing poor minority schools to close predisposes the students to serious academic and psychological adjustment problems and compounds their already high probability of school problems and failure.[27]

Given the nature and structure of education in the United States, it should not be at all surprising that the residents of working-class and minority neighborhoods have been forced to carry the disproportionate or exclusive burdens resulting from the transition of students from closed to receiving schools. Based on historical educational inequities and the racial and class stratification characteristic of U.S. society, it can be predicted that working-class minority schools will be forced to carry the exclusive, or near exclusive, burden of school closures.[28]

This prediction is based on several premises. First, there are conscious efforts on the part of school boards to prevent white students from fleeing the public schools into private schools or other public school systems, an option which is not available to poor families. Second, the class orientation of white, middle and upper-middle class dominated school boards is more sympathetic to the white constituency than to the ethnic minority constituency. Third, there is the desegregation argument and strategy. Many educators and school board members believe that school closures in segregated districts contribute to breaking down racial isolation and see desegregation under such circumstances as a desirable goal. There are several possible strategies for implementing desegregation in closure cases. One can desegregate by closing white schools and busing the students to minority schools, or closing minority schools and busing the students to white schools, or a plan combining these two strategies. In reality, the more frequently implemented plan is to close minority schools with one-way busing of minority students to white schools. This procedure places the exclusive burden of desegregation on minority students, however, and raises equity concerns. This issue has been of such magnitude that minority plaintiffs have filed racial discrimination lawsuits in Nashville, Phoenix, and Santa Barbara.[29]

Singling out and closing poor minority schools can be described as a "new form of denial" to equal educational opportunity.[30] On top of traditional forms of denial such as inequalities in school financing, unfavorable teachers' attitudes, cultural exclusion, a new method has surfaced—the elimination of neighborhood schools for minorities.

Is there empirical evidence that the closure of minority schools in segregated districts and the subsequent transition constitute obstacles to equal educational opportunity? The literature on this question is very sparse. There is one report, however, stemming from a Phoenix, Arizona school closure court case that sheds light on the equity issue.[31] In the 1982 *Castro* case, Black and Chicano parents and students brought suit against the

Phoenix Union High School District, charging racial discrimination in that their school was unfairly selected for closure. The plaintiffs argued that their school, Phoenix Union, a 94 percent minority inner-city high school was being singled out for closing, as well as two other predominantly minority high schools, while none of the district's six white schools were selected. As a result of the three minority school closures, a 30-square-mile area of the inner city contained no high school to serve the predominantly minority population.

After a lengthy hearing for injunctive relief, a federal court judge ruled in favor of the plaintiffs, concluding that the closing of Phoenix Union was discriminatory and had a negative impact upon the plaintiffs' rights to an equal educational opportunity. Phoenix Union was not to be closed. The present author, who served as the expert witness for the plaintiffs, presented extensive testimony with respect to potential impact on the displaced minority students. The author drew from several theoretical and empirical bases in the psychological and educational literature to illuminate the issue of alleged adverse impact. The major conclusion of the testimony was that the closure of Phoenix Union would generally create serious psychological and educational consequences for the students and limit their opportunities for equal education.

The ruling in favor of the plaintiffs in the *Castro* case could signal a critical development in the identification, analysis, and resolution of the equity issue. First, there is the legal implication. The finding in the *Castro* case regarding burden is very important for the advancement of school closure case law because: (a) the notion of burden became operational (for instance, the increased distance from home to school would negatively impact the extracurricular activity participation of minority students); (b) such burden would result in constitutional violation of students' rights for equal educational opportunity; (c) the judge specifically linked the issue of exclusiveness of burden and significant negative impact with the issue of budgetary problems.

Regarding this connection, the court found:

> The students, parents and public expect and have a right to expect that the administration of the schools of this city will be done fairly, without discrimination or undue adverse impact to any particular segment of the student population. The law requires nothing less. The School Board is not permitted to solve its budgetary problems by acts which result in undue burdens being placed exclusively on minorities, and excluding the majority students from like burdens.[32]

In reference to the judge's ruling on the burden notion and school closures in racially segregated school districts, the policy implication for equal educational opportunity one could draw from the finding in *Castro* is clear: in the management of declining school systems, the burden and sacrifice should be shared. Legally anything else is unacceptable.

Second, there is the equal educational opportunity policy consideration with respect to the schooling process itself. As a result of the *Castro* decision, it would behoove policy makers to be aware of the potentially serious disruptions closures create for high risk minorities. This contention should be considered in developing policy and management guidelines before closure decisions.

In conclusion, the available evidence surrounding the equity issue and school closures strongly suggests that retrenchment policies in segregated districts are not "color blind" nor are they free of class inequities. On the contrary, there is convincing documentation from several case studies of multi-ethnic communities and from a landmark court decision that school districts do not proceed fairly in their closure decision making. Furthermore, by all indications, such decisions exacerbate the already difficult conditions minority students face in their efforts to achieve a semblance of equal educational opportunity.

PUBLIC SUPPORT ISSUE

There is a connection between school closures and a potential decrease in community support for public schools. First, neighborhood schools are nearby. They are convenient for students and parents. Second, there is a political cohesion of local groups around their schools. Thus, it is not surprising that the school closure literature is full of reports in which parents have become quite annoyed when their schools were closed. The important question, however, is this: what are parents' options in expressing their dissatisfaction, and to what degree will these undermine the public schools? The evidence is skimpy on this issue, but the existing literature reports that school closings lead to community protest over closures before, during, and after, and such protest often results in varying expressions and messages that support for public education will no longer be forthcoming.[33]

Two of the gravest opposition tactics parents can use and have used in closure situations are: (a) voting down school levies, and (b) transfering their children from the public schools into private schools. These two forms of diminished lack of support for public education are particularly distressful to school districts because they undermine finances at a time of financial stringency. For example, in a comprehensive investigation of the neighborhood impact of school closures in Seattle, it was found that voting patterns on a school levy differed significantly between neighborhoods that had and had not experienced school closures. In those neighborhoods that had not undergone closings, 81.4 percent of the voters voted yes on the last school levy, while 68.3 percent of the voters voted yes in the neighborhoods whose schools had been closed.[34] In further regression analysis, however, results showed most of the variance was accounted for by race, sex, and age, thus indicating that community opposition to closures is highly complex.

The issue of parents who transfer their children from public schools to private schools has caused great alarm for public education. Although the exodus is part of a wider pattern of parental dissatisfaction with the public schools, closures or planned closures in some cases have precipitated the transfers. There are scattered reports that this is occurring. For example, in Wellesley, Massachusetts the bitter debates over planned and actual school closings in the 1970s frustrated some parents to the point that they withdrew their children and turned to private schooling.[35]

There is also some evidence that school districts have taken the offensive in closure situations to prevent students from fleeing to private schools. A case in point is Santa

Barbara, California in 1979. Of the 11 elementary schools in the district (five predominantly white schools, five predominantly Chicano, and one ethnically balanced), three Chicano schools were closed. The district was explicit in its criteria for closure proposal as to why no white schools were closed. In referring to one of the white schools, the district proposal noted:

> The school's residential area is the highest socioeconomic area in the city. Maintaining this area as a predominantly public school attendance area is important to the District. Unless the District can attract and hold these upper middle class areas, the entire Elementary School District is in danger of becoming more progressively ethnically and socioeconomically segregated.[36]

In short, the school district in Santa Barbara protected itself from receiving this threat from the white schools: "if you close our schools, we will move out and you will lose even more money because of additional declines in enrollment."

Another related aspect of the public support issue is the potential negative impact school closures have on decreased parental involvement in their children's schooling when their children enroll in receiving schools, which can be interpreted as a form of diminished support for schools. In a study of the minority school closures in Santa Barbara it was found that parental involvement across 10 different activity categories, such as participating in the Parent Teacher Association, parent teacher conferences, school board meetings, and field trips was higher in frequency in the pre-closure schools compared to the receiving schools.[37] Across the 10 categories, there was a 29 percent decline in participation frequency. The majority of the reasons parents gave for higher involvement levels at the pre-closure schools clustered around a "community" dimension—cultural activities, distance from home to school, and sense of neighborhood.

In summary, it appears that the available evidence pertinent to the public support issue raises a serious policy implication. The widespread dissatisfaction with schooling, erosion of support for public schools, and mistrust in school officials are, in some cases, exacerbated by school closures. Therefore, the social costs of closings should be weighted heavily in closure decision making. If parents reduce their political support for public schools and send their children to private schools in response to closure of a local school, any projected savings from closure may be illusory.

CONCLUSIONS

This brief review of school closures and policy issues permits a major conclusion. The limited research on the four closure aspects discussed in the paper provides little evidence that school closings are always in the best interests of school officials, teachers, parents, and students. On the contrary, school closures may be highly counterproductive. School officials should consider the issues raised here of school size, cost savings, equity, and public support in the development of policy prior to closings.

It appears that school officials and policy makers have been asking the wrong question during the era of retrenchment. As Shakeshaft and Gardner point out: "The dilemma of decline is not whether, or even how, to close a school, but rather how to finance the educational mission of the school district."[38]

To resolve this dilemma, school districts must hurdle the two barriers of fuzzy educational mission and negative mind sets toward decline. According to Shakeshaft and Gardner, districts must have clear, shared missions and have positive, visionary attitudes toward change. What alternatives to closing schools are there? How can the educational mission be financed? A number of proposals and actual experiences have been offered. These include the concept of decentralized mini-schools, various forms of shared space/lease arrangements with community and business interests, innovative new educational programs, and partnerships with business and industry.[39] For example, in St. Louis Park (Minnesota), the local school district is earning nearly $30,000 monthly income from rentals of empty school space. In Maryland, a school district produced an annual profit of $350,000 in 1981 in a leasing program.[40] By thinking creatively, opportunity can be found in the adversity of decline.

On a final point, it should be noted that a "baby boomlet" will be cresting in our elementary schools during the 1980s in many states. For example, it is predicted that California public schools will enroll an additional 309,000 elementary students by 1987–88 and another 556,000 by 1992–93, requiring 1,200 new schools by 1992.[41] In contrast, the high school enrollment will continue to decline nationally, but by the beginning of the next decade enrollment is projected to shift upward. As one researcher has admonished, if school officials are wise in thinking ahead to the 1990s, they will retain their schools today.[42]

NOTES

This article is a revision of "School Closures and Policy Issues" (policy paper no. 84-C3), published by the Institute for Research on Educational Finance and Governance at Stanford University.

1. W.L. Boyd, "The Politics of Declining Enrollments and School Closings," in N.H. Cambron-McCabe and A. Odden (eds.), *The Changing Politics of School Finance* (Cambridge, MA: Ballinger, 1982), pp. 231–267.
2. Ibid., p. 232. The widespread public resistance to investing further money in education is best exemplified by the tax limitation movement (e.g., Proposition 13 in California) that swept the nation in the late 1970s and early 1980s.
3. Charles H. Levine, "More on Cutback Management: Hard Questions for Hard Times," *Public Administration Review* 39 (1979), pp. 179–183.
4. H.J. Scott, "Desegregation in Nashville: Conflicts and Contradictions in Preserving Schools in Black Neighborhoods," *Education and Urban Society* 15 (1983), pp. 235–244.
5. The most comprehensive review of the literature on declining enrollments is by R. Zerchykov, *A Review of the Literature and an Annotated Bibliography on Managing Decline in School Systems* (Boston, MA: Institute for Responsive Education, Boston University, 1982). Of the 250 studies reviewed, 57 deal with school closures.
6. Although the existing literature is mainly prescriptive, recent scholarship has become more theoretical and empirical. See, for example, the entire volumes of *Education and Urban Society* 15 (1983) and *Peabody Journal of Education* 60 (1983), which are devoted to current knowledge on enrollment declines and retrenchment management.
7. Zerchykov, p. viii.
8. W.F. Fox, "Reviewing Economies of Size in Education," *Journal of Educational Finance* 6 (1981), pp. 273–296.
9. P. Lindsay, "The Effect of High School Size on Student Participation, Satisfaction, and Attendance," *Educational Evaluation and Policy Analysis* 4 (1982), p. 57.

10. R.G. Barker and P.V. Gump, *Big School, Small School: High School Size and Student Behavior* (Stanford: Stanford University Press, 1964).
11. Lindsay, pp. 57–65.
12. See, for instance, J.G. Chambers, "An Analysis of School Size Under a Voucher System," *Educational Evaluation and Policy Analysis* 3 (1981), pp. 29–40; J.W. Guthrie, "Organizational Scale and School Success," *Educational Evaluation and Policy Analysis* 1 (1979), pp. 17–27; A. Summers and B.L. Wolfe, "Do Schools Make a Difference?" *American Economic Review* 77 (1977), pp. 639–652. For empirical studies suggesting a negative relation between achievement and enrollment, see those studies cited by Chambers.
13. H.M. Levin, "Reclaiming Urban Schools; A Modest Proposal," *Policy Perspectives*, Stanford University, Institute for Research on Educational Finance and Governance (Winter 1983), p. 2.
14. J.I. Goodlad, *A Place Called School: Prospects for the Future* (New York: McGraw-Hill, 1984).
15. Ibid., p. 310.
16. Barker and Gump, p. 202.
17. Lindsay, p. 64.
18. C. Shakeshaft and D.W. Gardner, "Declining to Close Schools: Alternatives for Coping with Enrollment Decline," *Phi Delta Kappan* 64 (1983), pp. 492–496.
19. Levin, p. 2. Also see J. Stinchcombe, *Response to Declining Enrollment: School-Closing in Suburbia* (Lanham, MD: University Press of America, 1984), p. 271.
20. Shakeshaft and Gardner, p. 494.
21. R. Weatherly, B.J. Narver, and R. Elmore, "Managing the Politics of Decline: School Closures in Seattle," *Peabody Journal of Education* 60 (1983), pp. 10–24.
22. R.L. Andrews, *The Environmental Impact of School Closures* (1984, ERIC Document Reproduction Service No. ED 112 521).
23. Shakeshaft and Gardner, p. 495.
24. Ibid., p. 492.
25. W.L. Boyd and D.R. Wheaton, "Conflict Management in Declining School Districts," *Peabody Journal of Education* 60 (1983), p. 31.
26. See: D. Colton and A. Frelich, "Enrollment Decline and School Closings in a Large City," *Education and Urban Society* 11 (1979), pp. 396–417; Richard R. Valencia, "The School Closure Issue and the Chicano Community," *The Urban Review* 12 (1980), pp. 5–21; J. Dean, "Neighborhood Impacts of School Closings: The Case in New York City," *Education and Urban Society* 15 (1983), pp. 245–254; H.J. Scott, pp. 235–244; Richard R. Valencia, *Understanding School Closures: Discriminatory Impact on Chicano and Black Students* (Policy Monograph Series, No. 1, Stanford University: Stanford Center for Chicano Research, 1984).
27. Valencia, "The School Closure Issue."
28. Ibid.
29. See references in note 26.
30. Valencia, "The School Closure Issue."
31. Valencia, *Understanding School Closures*.
32. Ibid., p. 100.
33. M.A. Berger, "Neighborhood Schools: The New (?) Legal Response to Enrollment Decline and Desegregation," *Urban Education* 18 (1983), pp. 7–28.
34. Mathematica Policy Research, Seattle Washington; Seattle Public Schools, Washington, *Schools and Neighborhoods Research Study: The Neighborhood Survey. Final Report* (1976, ERIC Document Reproduction Service No. ED 133 914).
35. R.A. Bumstead, "Public or Private: What Parents Want From Their Schools," *Principal* 61 (1982), pp. 39–43.
36. Valencia, "The School Closure Issue," p. 10.
37. Richard R. Valencia, "The School Closure Issue and the Chicano Community: A Follow-up Study of the *Angeles* Case," *The Urban Review* (in press).

38. Shakeshaft and Gardner, p. 493.
39. See, for example, Goodlad, *A Place Called School*, p. 310.
40. Shakeshaft and Gardner, p. 493.
41. M. Fallon, "Baby-Boom Children Will Swell California System, Analyst Says," *Education Week* 3 (1984), p. 11.
42. Shakeshaft and Gardner, p. 493.